ISLAND NATURALS COOKBOOK

Written by Gina Franchini
Illustrations by Zoe Franchini

Published by Island Naturals, Hilo, Hawaii

Copyright © 2011
Island Naturals
Revised Second Printing, February 2012
Revised Third Printing, March 2013

Written by Gina Franchini
Illustrations by Zoe Franchini
Photos by Russell Ruderman & Gina Franchini
Front Cover Art © Island Naturals
Back Cover Art "Kupono" by Patricia Leo:
www.leosart.com

All rights reserved. No part of this book may be reproduced in any form, except for the inclusion of brief quotations in review, without permission in writing from the author/publisher.

ISBN 978-0-578-09676-6

Published by Island Naturals
Printed in U.S. by Instantpublisher.com

*To Ritsuko Tokura-Ellsworth,
with much gratitude.*

Rikko was our Hilo Kitchen Manager for our first 12 years until her retirement in 2010. The stores reflect the commitment, the integrity, the vision and the skill with which she helped shape Island Naturals.
--RR

To my family and friends.
Thanks for making life good!
--GF

ISLAND NATURALS LOCATIONS

HILO
Centrally located downtown at the Hilo Shopping Center, our Hilo location is a hub of town activity.
1221 Kilauea Avenue, Hilo, HI 96720
Phone: (808) 935-5533
Email: inhilo@islandnaturals.com

PAHOA
Conveniently located just off the main street in downtown Pahoa. Come see our beautiful indoor mural and our amazing old Pahoa garden.
15-1870 Akeakamai Loop, Pahoa, HI 96778
Phone: (808) 965-8322
Email: inpahoa@islandnaturals.com

KAILUA-KONA
We're just off Queen Kaahumanu Highway, a mile north of Ali'i Drive in the Old Industrial Area.
74-5487 Kaiwi Street, Kailua-Kona, HI 96740
Phone: (808) 326-1122
Email: inkona@islandnaturals.com

Please visit our website at:
www.islandnaturals.com

AN INTRODUCTION

Thank you for purchasing the Island Naturals Cookbook! We have resized many of our most popular recipes in smaller portions for use in your home. We have won many awards for our cooking, and the biggest award of all is the loyal customers we see every day at our stores. Often we're asked how we make certain dishes, and how we make our food taste so good. The answer - we use the best quality, freshest ingredients, preferably local and organic, and cook with care and aloha. That's our secret in a nutshell!

Our dishes range from American comfort foods, to Hawaiian specialties, Asian dishes, Mexican, European, and other ethnic influences from around the world. We do not limit ourselves to only one rule for food, so you will see vegetarian choices, meat and fish dishes, raw foods, smoothies and salads, healthy desserts, alternatives to meat, dairy, and gluten, and decadent indulgences. Our philosophy has always been to provide the widest range of choices, and let the customers choose.

This makes our cookbook useful to a wide variety of people. Being in Hawaii, we naturally include lots of local ingredients and ethnic influences from around the world. We hope you enjoy our Island Naturals Cookbook!

-Russell Ruderman, President and Founder

Let's get cooking...

At Island Naturals, our cooks prepare each dish for hundreds of people and thus a wide variety of palates. We imagine your cooking experiences will be for a more intimate audience.

With this in mind, please think of these recipes as a guideline and not law. These recipes have room for you to improvise. Maybe that means more spice, or less. Maybe you love garlic; then add more. Please, by all means, make adjustments.

Remember though, add small amounts of spice at a time as you can always continue to add, but you may not be able to tone down a dish as easily.

Please use organic ingredients in all your cooking. Organic is best for your health and the health of the planet. And it tastes better!

Look for vegan, gluten-free and raw recipe options. Please be sure that the ingredients meet your dietary criteria. Do your homework on specific ingredients. For instance, use a gluten-free soy sauce and cornstarch.

We encourage you to enter the kitchen with creativity, boldness and a good sense of humor! Cooking is, after all, a bit of chemistry, an act of love, and at least a few dirty dishes.

Have fun and let us know how it goes for you.

Table of Contents

Dressings & Marinades

Flax Seed Oil Dressing	∨ GF R	3
Ginger Mint Dressing	∨ GF R	4
Oil-Less Dressing	∨ GF	5
Shiitake Mushroom Marinade	∨ GF	7
Dill Marinade	GF	8
Garlic Chili Marinade	∨ GF	8
Honey Dijon Marinade	∨ GF	9
Thai Peanut Marinade	∨ GF	9
Nori Shoyu Marinade	∨ GF	10

Sauces & Gravies

Ancho Chili Sauce	∨ GF	12
Marinara Sauce	∨ GF	14
Pesto	GF	16
Peanut Sauce	∨ GF	17
Sweet Chili Sauce	∨ GF	18
Teriyaki Sauce	∨ GF	19
Sweet & Sour Sauce	∨ GF	20
Vegan Southern-Style Gravy	∨ GF	21
Cashew Gravy	∨ GF	22

Appetizers

Hummus	V GF	24
Mushroom Paté	V GF	25
Roasted Bell Pepper Tapenade	GF	26
Salsa	V GF R	27
Vegan Guacamole	V GF R	28
Roasted Red Pepper Tofu Dip	V GF	29
Artichoke Spinach Dip	GF	30
Olive Tapenade	V GF R	31
Bruschetta	V	32
Chimichurri	V GF R	33

Salads

Beets Salad	V GF	35
Cold Noodle Salad	V	36
Couscous Salad	V	37
Dill Potato Salad	V GF	38
Vegan Potato Salad	V GF	39
Island Sweet Potato Salad	V GF	40
Greek Pasta Salad	V GF	41
Pasta Salad	V GF	42
Green Papaya Salad	V GF R	44
Pickled Papaya Salad	V GF R	45
Seaweed Salad	V GF	46
Hijiki Seaweed Salad	V GF R	47
Fiesta Bean Salad	V GF	48
Mix Bean Salad	V GF	49
Quinoa Salad	V GF	50
Warabi Salad	V GF	51

Heart of Palm Salad   V GF R   52
Tabouli   V GF   53

Soups

Indian Potato Soup   V GF   55
Quinoa Soup   V GF   57
Vegan Corn Chowder   V   59
Roux 101   61
Vegan Ham & Bean Soup   V   62
Creamy Leek Soup   V GF   63
Vegan Potato Leek Soup   V   65
Miso Soup   V GF   66
Delightful Lima Bean Soup   V GF   67
Mushroom Barley Soup   V   69

Light Fare

Spring Rolls   V GF   72
Tofu Meatless Balls   V   73
Walnut Tofu Balls   V   74
Tofu Nuggets   V   75
Summer Rolls   V GF   77
Polenta Pizza   V GF   79
Eggplant Pockets   V GF   81
Seaweed Ahi Poke   GF R   82
Mac Nut Ahi Poke   GF R   82
Tofu Poke   V GF   83
Thai Tofu Salad   V GF   84

Chicken & Turkey Entrées

Chicken Enchiladas	GF	95
Coconut Chicken	GF	98
Tandoori Chicken	GF	100
Chicken Katsu		102
Indian Chicken Curry	GF	103
Thai Chicken Satay	GF	105
Sherry Chicken		107
Chicken Mole	GF	109
Turkey Meat Loaf	GF	110

Fish Entrées

Island Naturals Alaskan Salmon	GF	112
Fish Stew		113
Stuffed Bell Peppers		115
Salmon Croquettes		117
Island Naturals Lau Lau	GF	119

Vegetarian Entrées

Eggplant Parmesan	GF	122
Lasagna	GF	124
Savory Tofu	V GF	126
Moroccan Stew	V GF	128
Calzones		130
Goma-Dare Tofu	V GF	132
Pad Thai	V GF	133

Side Dishes

Garlic Rosemary Roasted Potatoes	V GF	136
Asian Rice Pilaf	V GF	137
Preparing Basmati Rice		138
Island Naturals Fry Rice	V GF	140
Mexican Rice	V GF	142
Thai Curry Rice	V GF	143

Baked Goods & Desserts

Island Naturals Granola	V	146
Scones	V	148
Jalapeño Cheddar Pull Aparts		150
Tapioca Pudding	V GF	152
Sweet Potato Tapioca Pudding	V GF	153
Vegan Banana Cake	V	154
Island Naturals Carrot Cake	V	155
Vegan Cream Cheese Frosting	V GF	157
Vegan Chocolate Frosting	V GF	158
Vegan Chocolate Cake	V	159
Raw Chocolate Truffles	V GF R	161
Vegan Date Squares	V	162
Raw Mint Marble Pie	V GF R	164
Summer Berry Purée	V GF R	167
Vegan Pumpkin Pie	V GF	168

Drinks & Smoothies

Ginger Juice	∨ GF R	171
Lemongrass Juice	∨ GF	172
Island Naturals Classic Smoothies:		173
Green Goo	∨ GF R	173
Berry Builder	∨ GF R	174
Immune Me	∨ GF R	174
Get Mental	∨ GF R	174
Energy Eruption	∨ GF R	175
Hot Cold Buster	∨ GF R	175
Chill Out	∨ GF R	175
Jungle Jive	∨ GF R	176
Create Your Own	∨ GF R	176

Index	177
Acknowledgements	183

∨ — vegan or with a vegan option
GF — gluten-free or with a GF option
R — raw food or with a raw option

Island Naturals Recipes

*One cannot think well, love well,
sleep well, if one has not dined well.*

—Virginia Woolf

Dressings & Marinades

Flax Seed Oil Dressing	∨ GF R	3
Ginger Mint Dressing	∨ GF R	4
Oil-Less Dressing	∨ GF	5
Shiitake Mushroom Marinade	∨ GF	7
Dill Marinade	GF	8
Garlic Chili Marinade	∨ GF	8
Honey Dijon Marinade	∨ GF	9
Thai Peanut Marinade	∨ GF	9
Nori Shoyu Marinade	∨ GF	10

FLAX SEED OIL DRESSING

This is a fabulous dressing for your favorite salad. Mix it up in a canning jar or bottle with a tight fitting lid. Shake well and dress those greens. Yields 2 cups

- ¼ medium onion, chopped
- 2 cloves garlic, minced
- 1 bunch (about 1 overflowing cup) fresh parsley, coarsely chopped
- 1 tbsp Italian seasoning
- ¼ cup raw sugar
- ¼ tsp white pepper
- ¼ cup water
- ¼ cup rice vinegar
- ½ cup flax seed oil
- ½ cup safflower or olive oil

Combine the onion, garlic, parsley, Italian seasoning, sugar and pepper in a bowl.

Put water, vinegar and oils directly into blender. Give it a quick whirl. Add the dry ingredients and blend until smooth—30 seconds or so.

Store in the refrigerator.

GINGER MINT DRESSING

This dressing is delightful and easy to make. A fresh alternative to bottled dressings.
Yields 3 cups

	¾ cup raw sugar
	1 tbsp salt
	1 tsp white pepper
	2 bunches of mint, chopped
	2 tbsp (about a thumb-sized piece) fresh ginger, chopped
	½ medium yellow onion, chopped
	¼ cup ground mustard
	¼ cup olive or safflower oil
	2 tbsp water
	2 tbsp apple cider vinegar

In a small mixing bowl, combine the sugar, salt and pepper. Set aside.

Place the mint, ginger, onion, and mustard directly into a blender. Pulse until paste-like. Add sugar mixture from bowl. Blend briefly to combine.

Add oil, water and vinegar.

Blend until smooth.

Keep refrigerated.

OIL-LESS DRESSING

Don't limit this truly lovely dressing to only salad greens; try it over steamed or raw vegetables of your choice. Refrigerate leftovers.
Yields about 2 ½ cups

  ½ medium onion, chopped
  3-4 cloves garlic, to taste, minced
  ½ stalk celery, chopped
  3-4 sprigs fresh parsley, coarsely chopped
  5-7 leaves fresh basil, coarsely chopped
  dash of ground ginger
  ½ cup raw sugar
  2 tbsp stone ground mustard
  1 tsp each: Spike seasoning, dried thyme,
     paprika, dried marjoram, Italian seasoning
  ½ tsp allspice
  ½ tsp ground black pepper

  ¾ cup apple cider vinegar
  ¼ cup balsamic vinegar
  2 tbsp fresh lime juice
  2 tbsp soy sauce
  Up to ¼ cup vegetable broth or water, to
     taste
  dash of salt, to taste

Combine first set of ingredients (from the onion to the black pepper) in large bowl or directly in a blender. Pulse until smooth.

Add vinegars, lime juice and soy sauce. Pulse to combine. Taste test. Thin with broth or water to taste. Salt to taste.

Chill.

MARINADES

Want to turn tonight's dinner into something special? Just whip up any one of these amazing marinades. Each recipe makes enough marinade for roughly 4 – 6 pieces of chicken or fish fillets or 1 pound of tofu. (For the out of the ordinary, the marinades can be used for lamb, tempeh or seasonal vegetables as well.) Adjust seasoning to your taste.

Simply combine ingredients in a bowl. Whisk together for good measure and any one of these marinades is ready to use. (Only a few require a bit more effort.) Brush on or pour over your choice of meat or tofu arranged in an oven-safe pan. Marinade time is flexible. You can prepare ahead and marinade all day or when time is short, toss it all together and throw it in the oven.

SHIITAKE SESAME MARINADE

This marinade is worth the few extra steps. You can thin the broth with water if it is too strong for your taste.

    8 - 10 pieces dried shiitake mushrooms
    2 cups water
    ¼ cup Braggs amino acids
    ¾ cup lime juice
    ½ tsp chopped garlic
    ½ tsp ground ginger
    2 tbsp fresh cilantro, chopped
    dash chili flakes

Place shiitake mushrooms in saucepan and cover with water. Bring to a boil. Reduce heat and simmer until half the water is absorbed. Remove from heat and cool. Strain into a bowl, reserving the broth. Mince mushrooms and set aside.

In a small bowl, combine Braggs, lime juice, garlic, ginger and cilantro. Stir well. Add mushroom broth, minced mushrooms and chili flakes.

Pour marinade over your meat or tofu arranged in a baking pan. Bake until done.

DILL MARINADE

This creamy marinade offers a particularly perfect marriage with salmon.

½ cup sour cream
½ cup heavy cream
2 tbsp fresh dill, chopped
½ tsp garlic powder
salt and pepper to taste

GARLIC CHILI MARINADE

You will be wowed by the symphony of flavors in this marinade.

1 cup sweet chili sauce
2 tbsp garlic, chopped
¼ cup peanuts, chopped
1 tbsp ginger, chopped
¼ cup soy sauce (shoyu)
¼ cup cilantro, chopped
salt & pepper

HONEY DIJON MARINADE

A nice delicately sweet marinade.

    ¼ cup honey
    1 cup dijon mustard
    ¼ cup white wine
    ¼ tbsp salt & pepper

THAI PEANUT MARINADE

A very easy marinade for which you will find limitless uses.

    2 cloves garlic, minced
    1 thumb sized piece ginger, minced
    ¾ tsp crushed red pepper
    ¼ + 1 tbsp cup peanut butter
    ¼ cup soy sauce
    1 cup ketchup
    scant ½ cup coconut milk
    1 tsp safflower or peanut oil

Dry roast garlic, ginger, and red pepper over low heat, until browned. Remove from heat and add to a bowl or jar. Add remaining ingredients. Mix or shake.

NORI SHOYU MARINADE

A most tempting marinade with Asian influences.

8 sheets nori
½ cup ginger, chopped
½ c toasted sesame seeds
½ cup garlic, chopped
2 cups shoyu
1 cup sugar
2 tbsp red chili flakes

Put nori sheets in food processor or blender. Pulse to break down to dime size chunks. Add remaining ingredients. Pulse a few times to combine.

Sauces & Gravies

Ancho Chili Sauce	∨ GF	12
Marinara Sauce	∨ GF	14
Pesto	GF	16
Peanut Sauce	∨ GF	17
Sweet Chili Sauce	∨ GF	18
Teriyaki Sauce	∨ GF	19
Sweet & Sour Sauce	∨ GF	20
Vegan Southern-Style Gravy	∨ GF	21
Cashew Gravy	∨ GF	22

ANCHO CHILI SAUCE

Use this fabulous recipe over fish, chicken or our enchiladas. This recipe makes a big batch, but we are convinced you will be glad for that! It keeps well in a glass jar in the fridge or freezer.
Yields about 4 Cups

- 2-3 seeded ancho or chipotle peppers (or ½ of both), chopped
- 2 tbsp olive oil
- ½ stalk celery, chopped
- ½ medium onion, chopped
- ½ medium carrot, chopped
- 2-4 cloves garlic, chopped
- 1 tsp salt
- 3 cups chicken or unchicken broth
- ¼ cup olive oil
- ½ cup masa or masa harina (traditional Mexican corn flour)

Split peppers and remove stem and seeds. Chop and set aside. Be mindful, as pepper oils will burn skin and eyes. Wash hands thoroughly.

In a medium saucepan, sauté celery, onion, carrots and garlic in oil, about 5 minutes. Add salt. Add peppers and broth. Lightly boil over medium low heat, until vegetables soften, about 10 minutes.

Meanwhile, in a small bowl, whisk the oil and masa together until smooth. Slowly add to sauce, stirring constantly to avoid clumping.

Remove from heat.

Puree sauce with a hand mixer or in batches in a blender until smooth.

It's ready to use.

MARINARA SAUCE

A good marinara sauce is key to any good Italian dish. Make a double batch and freeze half for next time. Fresh herbs are key, but dried herbs will do in a pinch.
Yields 3 cups

¼ cup olive oil
2 tsp Italian seasoning
1 small yellow onion, finely chopped
1 green bell pepper, finely chopped
Several sprigs fresh Italian parsley, finely chopped
¼ cup red wine
2 sprigs fresh marjoram, finely chopped
handful fresh basil, finely chopped
2 cups (16 oz) diced tomato
1 cup (8 oz) tomato puree
½ cup (4 oz) tomato paste
salt & pepper to taste

In a large pot, heat olive oil over medium high heat. Add Italian seasoning. Add onion, bell pepper and parsley and sauté for 3-5 minutes, until lightly browned. Add wine and herbs. Stir in all tomatoes. Salt and pepper to taste.

Simmer over low heat for 2-4 hours. Longer cook time will enhance the melding of flavors for a delectable marinara sauce.

Enjoy the smells and tastes of Italy!

PESTO

Pesto is yet another versatile and classic recipe. Play with the recipe until you get it just right for you. Remember the garlic is raw and powerful, so start with less and work up from there.
Yields 2 cups

¼ cup pine nuts, roasted
2 cups fresh sweet basil
½ cup Parmesan cheese
2+ cloves garlic, to taste
pinch of salt
¼ cup olive oil

Dry roast pine nuts in oven on low temperature or in a pan on the stove until lightly browned. Do not over roast. Let cool.

Pulse basil, cooled pine nuts, half of the Parmesan cheese, garlic and salt in food processor. Slowly add oil through feeder.

Scrape into a bowl and stir in remaining cheese. Adjust oil, as needed.

Tips: You can replace the pine nuts with sunflower seeds, walnuts or macadamia nuts.

Gluten Free Option: Do not dry roast pine nuts. Use other raw nuts or seeds of your choice.

PEANUT SAUCE

This spicy sauce is a perfect match for our Thai Chicken Satay. It is also great with our Summer Rolls. Quick and impressive!
Yields about 1 ½ cups

    ¼ cup peanut butter
    ½ cup ketchup
    ¼ cup Sweet Chili Sauce (see pg 18)
    ½ cup coconut milk
    1 tsp+ fresh lime juice, to taste
    a pinch cumin
    ¼ cup hot water

Combine all ingredients in medium bowl. Stir or whisk to combine.

Serve.

SWEET CHILI SAUCE

Making your own Sweet Chili Sauce is so easy and rewarding. This is a wonderful accompaniment for any Thai cuisine. You'll definitely want some for dipping Summer Rolls and Spring Rolls.
Yields about ½ cup

¼ cup water
½ cup + 2 tbsp raw sugar
½ tsp salt
3 cloves garlic, minced
3 tsp ginger, minced
½ tbsp chili pepper flakes, adjust to taste (1 tbsp is spicy-hot)
1 ½ tbsp cornstarch
3-4 tbsp cool water, for dissolving cornstarch
½ cup rice vinegar

Add water, sugar, salt, garlic, ginger and chili flakes to a saucepan. Bring to boil over medium-high heat.

In a small bowl whisk cornstarch into water until well combined. Add to pot slowly. Stir to combine. Remove from heat. Add vinegar. Mix and chill.

TERIYAKI SAUCE

This may become your go-to sauce. Use as a marinade for grilled meats, fish and vegetables. Try a teriyaki burger with pineapple. Anything goes. Yields about 5 cups

- 4 cups soy sauce
- 2 ½ cups raw sugar
- 2 tbsp green onion, chopped
- 2 tbsp ginger, chopped
- 3 cloves garlic, chopped
- ½ tsp chili pepper flakes
- 1 piece star anise
- ½ cup cornstarch
- ½ cup water, for dissolving cornstarch

Combine all ingredients except the cornstarch and water in a saucepan. Bring to a boil over high heat. Reduce heat to simmer.

While simmering, mix cornstarch and water in a small bowl. Whisk to combine.

Add cornstarch mixture to saucepan, stirring well. Turn off the heat. Allow to rest overnight or for several hours.

Strain and discard pulp. Put leftover sauce in a glass bottle with a tight seal and store in the refrigerator.

SWEET & SOUR SAUCE

An all-around tasty sauce. We recommend serving this over Tofu Meatless Balls.
Yields about 3 cups

1 cup ketchup
1 cup unsweetened pineapple juice
2 thumb size pieces of ginger, chopped
½ cup brown sugar
1 tbsp cornstarch
3 tbsp of water, for dissolving cornstarch
1 cup rice wine vinegar

Whisk all ingredients together. Bring to a boil over medium heat.

In a small bowl whisk cornstarch into water until well combined. Add to pot slowly, stirring to combine. Remove from heat. If you prefer, you can strain to remove ginger. Add vinegar. Mix and chill.

Keep extra in a tightly lidded jar in the fridge or freezer.

VEGAN SOUTHERN-STYLE GRAVY

A gluten-free, vegan and deliciously fast and easy gravy, this recipe is sure to become one of your favorite comfort foods. Serve atop your favorite starch or protein. Good enough for Thanksgiving dinner!
Yields about 3 cups

- 2 cups warm water
- ½ cup raw cashews
- 2 tbsp nutritional yeast flakes
- 2 tbsp soy sauce (gluten-free variety)
- 1 tbsp safflower oil
- 2 tsp onion powder
- 1 tsp Bakon Seasoning
- ½ tsp salt
- ½ tsp garlic powder
- ½ tsp ground coriander

Combine all ingredients in a blender and blend well for 3-4 minutes.

Put pureed gravy into a saucepan and simmer on medium low heat for 10 minutes.

Serve warm.

CASHEW GRAVY

This is a nutritious, non-dairy gravy perfect for feasts or otherwise. Spectacular every time! Yields about 3 cups

- 2 ½ cups filtered water
- scant ¾ cup cashew pieces
- 2 tbsp tapioca flour, arrowroot powder or cornstarch
- 2 tbsp Braggs
- 1 ½ tsp onion powder
- ½ tsp sea salt

Combine all ingredients in a blender. Blend until smooth.

Place in a double boiler on medium high heat and cook until thick.

(Don't let the double boiler scare you—if need be, just place a glass or stainless steel bowl over a larger pot partially filled with water. Don't let the water touch the bottom of the bowl. Keep water at a simmer. The trapped steam will heat the bowl.)

Serve warm.

Appetizers

Hummus — V GF — 24

Mushroom Paté — V GF — 25

Roasted Red Bell Pepper Tapenade — GF — 26

Salsa — V GF R — 27

Vegan Guacamole — V GF R — 28

Roasted Red Bell Pepper Tofu Dip — V GF — 29

Artichoke Spinach Dip — GF — 30

Olive Tapenade — V GF R — 31

Bruschetta — V — 32

Chimichurri — V GF R — 33

HUMMUS

Quick and easy, this simple recipe is a great dip with crackers or fresh veggies. It's also a scrumptious addition to any sandwich, wrap or the traditional falafel.
Yields 2 cups

    2 cups garbanzo beans*, cooked or canned
    ½ cup tahini
    ¼ cup olive oil
    ¼ cup fresh juice from a lime or lemon
    2 cloves garlic, minced
    1 tbsp cumin
    salt & pepper to taste
    2 tbsp fresh parsley, chopped (optional)

Place all ingredients, except parsley, in a blender or food processor. Combine well.

Try a bit and adjust to your taste preference by adding more seasoning, lemon or lime juice, or garlic as desired.

If desired, garnish with a swirl of olive oil, pinch of cumin and chopped parsley.

Store in refrigerator.

*With cooked beans, reserve some of the liquid to thin as needed. For canned, use water to thin.

MUSHROOM PATÉ

This delicious paté is packed full of protein—a nice change from ordinary dips often served at gatherings or potlucks. It is quite versatile as a dip with crackers, bread or crudités or as a spread on your favorite wrap or sandwich.
Yields 2 + cups

½ lb mushrooms of your choice, cleaned & trimmed
1 medium onion, chopped
3 cloves garlic, minced
1 tbsp olive oil
2 tbsp fresh basil, chopped
1 tsp fresh thyme
¼ cup tahini
1 ½ cups tofu, drained and crumbled
½ cup soy sauce

In a medium pan, sauté the mushrooms, onion and garlic in olive oil over medium high heat until onion is translucent, about 10 minutes. Set aside.

Crumble the tofu into a food processor or blender. Add the mushroom sauté. Add tahini. Blend until smooth. Add the basil, thyme and soy sauce. Pulse quickly a few times to combine.

Chill for an hour or two before serving.

Tip: While fresh is best, you may also substitute dried mushrooms. In which case, use about 10 whole dry shiitake mushrooms. Re-hydrate by placing mushrooms in a saucepan. Cover with water and boil until mushrooms are soft, about 5 minutes. Strain and cool. Proceed as above.

ROASTED BELL PEPPER TAPENADE

Four ingredients and one delicious outcome.
Serves 4-6

- 3 cups artichoke hearts
- ¼ cup Parmesan cheese
- 1 cup roasted bell peppers
- 1-2 tbsp olive oil

Put artichoke hearts, Parmesan cheese and roasted bell peppers in a food processor. Pulse while adding oil slowly until smooth.

Serve.

SALSA

Nothing beats fresh salsa! Think beyond chips and add salsa to tacos, guacamole, eggs and over grilled vegetables or meats. Why not plant a salsa garden?
Serves 4-6

- 3 lbs ripe tomatoes, diced
- ¼ red onion, diced
- ¼ cup fresh cilantro, chopped
- scant ¼ cup fresh lime juice
- 1 tsp cumin
- 1-2 tsp chili pepper flakes (more or less as desired)
- 2 cloves garlic, minced
- salt and pepper to taste

Combine all ingredients in large bowl.

Adjust flavor to your liking.

Allow salsa a bit of siesta time before serving.

VEGAN GUACAMOLE

A fresh and easy appetizer. A great compliment to just about anything—Mexican food, eggs, on sandwiches, baked potatoes...
Serves 4-6

- 2 medium ripe avocado, mashed
- ½ small red onion, diced
- 1 medium tomato, diced
- 2-4 tbsp fresh cilantro, chopped
- 1 tbsp lemon juice
- 1 tsp hot sauce (optional)
- 1 clove garlic, minced and to taste
- ¼ tsp ground cumin
- salt and pepper to taste

In a medium bowl, mash the avocadoes with a fork. Leave it a bit lumpy, avoiding a pureed consistency.

Add onion, tomato and cilantro. Mix in the lemon juice, hot sauce, garlic, cumin, salt and pepper.

It's ready! Indulge!

Tip: A friend of mine swears that leaving the avocado pit in the bowl keeps the guacamole fresh and vibrant.

ROASTED RED PEPPER TOFU DIP

Another versatile dip, high in protein and super easy to make. Serve it as a snack or as a light meal.
Serves 4-6

    1 lb tofu, drained
    2 tbsp rice wine vinegar
    2 tbsp olive oil
    1 cup roasted red peppers
    1 ½ tbsp nutritional yeast
    salt and pepper to taste

Crumble tofu into food processor.

Add remaining ingredients to food processor. Blend until silky and smooth.

It's that easy!

ARTICHOKE SPINACH DIP

This is a no-cook artichoke dip recipe. Serve with pita chips, tortilla chips or a sliced baguette. It is easy to prepare and always a hit!
Serves 4-6

3 cups artichoke hearts
2 cups frozen spinach, thawed & excess water squeezed
½ cup sour cream
½ cup mayonnaise or veganaise
¾ cup Parmesan cheese, grated
several sprigs of parsley, chopped
1 tsp garlic, minced
salt and pepper to taste

Drain the artichokes. Pulse in a food processor until chunky. (You may also chop the artichoke on a cutting board.)

Mix the rest of the ingredients in a medium serving bowl. Add chopped artichokes. Stir to combine.

Serve.

OLIVE TAPENADE

A densely flavorful accompaniment to crackers, crusted bread or crudités. Try using as a condiment on sandwiches or wraps. Add to pasta, potatoes or fish.
Yields about 2 cups

　　2 cups kalamata olives, pitted
　　¼ cup capers
　　4 – 6 cloves garlic, minced
　　1 tbsp dried oregano
　　2 tbsp fresh parsley, chopped
　　1 tbsp olive oil

Place all ingredients, except olive oil, into a food processor.

Pulse while slowly adding olive oil through feed. Do not over process. You want it well combined but with a slightly chunky consistency.

Serve.

BRUSCHETTA

A classic appetizer, bruschetta is impressive to the palate with its melding of simple, savory flavors.
Serves 4-6

- 6 medium tomatoes, diced
- 4 tbsp olive oil, divided
- 2 tbsp balsamic vinegar
- handful of fresh basil, chopped and divided
- 1 loaf French baguette or Italian bread
- 1 tbsp garlic, minced
- 1 ball fresh mozzarella cheese, thinly sliced (optional)

In a small mixing bowl, combine tomatoes, 2 tbsp of the olive oil, vinegar, and 2/3 of the basil.

Slice the bread into about inch-thick pieces. Mix remaining oil with garlic and rub onto each slice of bread. Arrange on a baking sheet.

Top each slice with the tomato mixture, then a slice of cheese. Sprinkle reserved basil over the top.

Toast at 425 degrees F, about 5 minutes until cheese melts and tomatoes are warm.
Serve right from the oven.

Tip: Try this version too: top the rubbed bread with a cheese slice and toast. Then spoon the tomato mixture onto the toast.

CHIMICHURRI

This recipe is an excellent dip served with chips or crackers, but don't limit yourself! Add it to your omelet, spread it on a burger, or use it as a marinade. Very versatile and delicious!
Yields about 2 cups

- 1 bunch parsley
- ¼ cup red wine vinegar
- ½ red onion, chopped
- 4 cloves garlic
- ½ red bell peppers, chopped
- 1 tbsp oregano
- 1 tbsp paprika
- ¼ cup fresh lime juice
- 1 ripe tomato, peeled and chopped in chunks

- ½ cup olive oil
- Salt and pepper to taste

Add first set of ingredients (from parsley to tomato) to a food processor. Pulse until everything is minced. Do not overdo it.

Slowly add the oil through the feeder and pulse until combined. Salt and pepper to taste.

If time allows, let sit for an hour or two for optimal flavor.

SALADS

Beets Salad	V GF	35
Cold Noodle Salad	V	36
Couscous Salad	V	37
Dill Potato Salad	V GF	38
Vegan Potato Salad	V GF	39
Island Sweet Potato Salad	V GF	40
Greek Pasta Salad	V GF	41
Pasta Salad	V GF	42
Green Papaya Salad	V GF R	44
Pickled Papaya Salad	V GF R	45
Ogo Seaweed Salad	V GF	46
Hijiki Seaweed Salad	V GF R	47
Fiesta Bean Salad	V GF	48
Mix Bean Salad	V GF	49
Quinoa Salad	V GF	50
Warabi Salad	V GF	51
Heart of Palm Salad	V GF R	52
Tabouli	V GF	53

BEETS SALAD

Many a great dish begins with the telltale deep red stain of beet juice on your fingertips, your cutting board, your kitchen towel...this is no exception. Serves 4-6

- 3 lbs beets
- dash of salt
- 3 tbsp sunflower seeds
- 3 tbsp walnuts, chopped
- 1 tsp fresh rosemary, chopped
- ¼ cup + 2 tbsp balsamic vinegar
- 3 tbsp olive oil
- salt & pepper to taste

Give the beets a good scrub. Add clean beets to a heavy stockpot and cover with water. Bring to a boil. Reduce heat to low and simmer for up to 45 minutes, or until beets are tender—similar to a potato. Drain.

While still hot, remove peel by running beets under water and rubbing peel away.

Cut the beets into small cubes and place in a large serving bowl.

Add remaining ingredients. Stir to evenly distribute.

Tip: Try adding some chopped fresh parsley and crumbled goat cheese.

COLD NOODLE SALAD

A quick and sensible dish, cold noodle salad takes next to no time to prepare. Great for lunches on the go or as a side with your favorite fish or tofu dish.
Serves 4-6

- 1 package long rice noodles
- 1 large carrot, peeled and julienned
- 1 red bell pepper, sliced
- 1 small piece ginger, peeled and thinly sliced
- 2 tbsp sweet chili sauce
- 1 tsp sesame oil
- 1 tsp soy sauce

Cook noodles as directed and cool.

Mix all ingredients in a large bowl.

Refrigerate. Serve cold.

COUSCOUS SALAD

This salad takes nearly no time at all to prepare. It is a colorful and lively addition to your cooking repertoire.
Serves 4-6

- 1 cup couscous
- 1 ¼ cup boiling water
- ½ cup orange juice
- 2 tbsp olive oil
- 2 cups garbanzo beans, cooked or canned & rinsed
- ½ red bell pepper, diced
- ½ cup raisins
- 2 tsp each fresh parsley and mint, chopped
- ¼ cup cucumber, seeded and diced
- ½ cup oranges, peeled and sliced into chunks
- salt and pepper to taste

Put the couscous in a large bowl. Measure the boiling water and add to bowl. Let the couscous soak up water, about 15 minutes. Fluff with a fork and put in a medium serving bowl.

Add orange juice and olive oil to couscous. Stir until well combined. Add remaining ingredients.

Mix gently to distribute evenly. Serve chilled or at room temperature.

DILL POTATO SALAD

A summertime barbeque favorite! The dill gives this potato salad a light and fresh taste.
Serves 4-6

   2 ½ lbs potatoes
   3 tbsp red onion, cut sliver
   2 tsp fresh parsley, chopped
   2 tsp fresh dill, chopped
   ½ cup of mayonnaise or veganaise
   2 tbsp of Dijon mustard
   salt and pepper to taste
   _____

Place cleaned whole potatoes in a large pot with enough water to cover plus a few inches. Boil until tender and peel starts to come away, about 20 minutes. Check for softness with a fork periodically. Cool and peel. Cut potatoes into bite size chunks.

In a large bowl, combine potatoes with remaining ingredients. Stir and serve.

Tip: Try leaving the peels on!

VEGAN POTATO SALAD

Enjoy potato salad any day of the week with this easy and delicious recipe. It's vegan, so make enough for everyone.
Serves 6-8

- 3 ½ lbs potatoes
- 3 tbsp red onion, cut into slivers
- ½ large carrot, grated
- ½ large red pepper, cut into slivers
- 2-4 tsp fresh parsley, chopped
- ¾ cup veganaise
- 3 tbsp mustard
- ½ tsp paprika
- salt & pepper to taste

Boil potatoes in a large pot until tender and peel starts to come away, about 20 minutes. Cool and peel. Cut potatoes into bite size chunks.

In a large bowl, combine potatoes with remaining ingredients.

Refrigerate before serving.

ISLAND SWEET POTATO SALAD

A tasty local version of this proverbial favorite. Purple sweet potatoes are a highly nutritious food—loaded with antioxidants, high in fiber and fat-free.
Serves 6-8

  3 lbs purple sweet potatoes
  1½ tbsp apple cider vinegar
  2 tbsp Bragg's amino acids
  ¼ cup mayonnaise or veganaise
  pinch crushed red pepper flakes
  ½ tsp garlic minced
  salt and pepper to taste
  ¼ cup red onion, diced
  ¼ cup celery, sliced thin
  2 tbsp fresh dill
  ½ red bell pepper, thinly sliced

Bring a large pot of water to a boil and add cleaned potatoes. Boil until tender, about 15 minutes. Strain and set aside to cool. Once cooled, remove peel. Cut into cubes.

Combine vinegar, mayonnaise, Braggs, red pepper flakes, garlic, salt and pepper in a large mixing bowl and whisk well.

Add onion, celery, dill, bell pepper and potatoes. Mix gently until evenly distributed.

GREEK PASTA SALAD

Flavorful and colorful! This is an easy make-ahead recipe giving the wonderful flavors time to linger. Works well with your favorite gluten-free pasta too. Serves 6-8

- 4 cups (1 lb) pasta, spirals or desired shape
- ¼ cup lime juice
- generous ¼ cup olive oil
- generous ½ cup sun dried tomatoes, soaked in hot water
- 1 cup roasted peppers, coarsely chopped
- ¼ cup capers
- 1 cup artichoke hearts, chopped
- ¾ cup green or black olives, sliced or coarsely chopped
- 2 tsp each fresh oregano, parsley and basil, chopped
- 2 tsp garlic, minced
- ½ cup feta cheese, crumbled
- salt and pepper to taste

Cook pasta, al dente. Strain. Add pasta to a large bowl and stir in lime juice and olive oil.

Add remaining ingredients to cooled pasta. Stir until veggies are distributed evenly.

If time allows, let flavors meld for a few hours before serving.

PASTA SALAD

This pasta salad will become a family favorite. Always great for on-the-go lunches at the beach. Serves 4-6

    4 cups (1 lb) pasta, fusilli or bow tie
    ½ of each: red, green and yellow bell pepper, diced
    ½ medium red onion, diced
    ¾ cup black olives, chopped
    ¾ cup artichoke hearts, chopped
    ¼ cup fresh parsley, chopped

DRESSING
    ½ cup fresh lime juice
    ¼ cup balsamic vinegar
    2 tbsp safflower oil
    2 tbsp olive oil
    2½ tsp Spike seasoning
    pinch white pepper
    salt to taste

———————————

Cook pasta, al dente. Strain and cool. In a large serving bowl, combine vegetables and cooled pasta.

Combine all dressing ingredients in a jar. Cover and shake. Add dressing to salad and marinate for at least 1 hour, stirring occasionally. Serve cold or at room temperature.

This goes for all pasta dishes—

Gluten-free Option: Substitute pasta made with rice, quinoa or corn flours or other gluten-free flours. Follow package directions and remember you want the pasta al dente—cooked long enough to be firm rather than soft—so that it will hold up in the salad.

Vegan Option: Omit cheese.

GREEN PAPAYA SALAD

Green papaya salad's fresh ingredients come together to create a delightfully light and pleasing salad.
Serves 4

    1 large green papaya, peeled & seeded
    1 medium carrot
    1 cup peanuts, roasted
    ½ cup purple cabbage, thinly sliced
    ½ medium red bell pepper, finely chopped
    ½ cup green onion, chopped
    1 tbsp garlic, minced
    ½ cup fresh lime juice
    pinch crushed red chili pepper
    3 tbsp Bragg's amino acid
    ½ cup agave syrup

Grate the papaya and carrot. Add to a medium serving bowl.

Roast peanuts in oven on low heat or on the stove over medium heat until golden brown. Set aside.

Add remaining ingredients to papaya and carrot. Stir gently. Top with roasted peanuts.

Tip: Replace peanuts with raw macadamia nuts or cashews.
Raw Food Option: Skip roasting of nuts.

PICKLED PAPAYA SALAD

This salad is a nice use for the abundant and beautiful non-GMO Hawaii papayas.
Serves 4

   1 large green papaya, peeled & seeded
   2 medium carrots
   ¼ cup raisins
   ½ medium red onion, diced
   ½ red bell pepper, diced
   1 cup apple cider vinegar
   ¾ cup raw sugar
   salt and pepper to taste

Grate the papaya and carrot. Add to a medium bowl with raisins, onion and bell pepper.

In a saucepan, mix vinegar and sugar. Bring to a boil over medium high heat, stirring until the sugar is dissolved. Pour immediately into the rest of the ingredients and mix gently. Salt and pepper.

Serve.

SEAWEED SALAD

If you aren't eating seaweeds, you are missing out on a delicious and healthy food. They are just packed full of vitamins and minerals. Enjoy your greens—your sea greens!
Serves 4

- 1 lb ogo seaweed
- dash of salt
- 1 red bell pepper, sliced
- ¼ red onion, sliced
- ¼ cup sesame seeds, roasted
- ¼ cup soy sauce
- 2 tbsp sesame oil
- ¼ cup rice vinegar
- ¼ cup green onion, chopped

Blanch the ogo—bring enough lightly salted water to cover the ogo to a boil in a medium saucepan. Add ogo and turn off heat. Drain and rinse in cold water.

Put cooled ogo in a medium bowl. Add remaining ingredients. Stir to distribute ingredients evenly.

Serve cold.

HIJIKI SEAWEED SALAD

Hijiki is a sea vegetable and a traditional Japanese food. It is rich in dietary fiber and minerals, including calcium, iron and magnesium.
Serves 4

1 cup hijiki seaweed
1 ¼ cups cold water

3 tbsp brown rice vinegar
1 tbsp sesame oil
3 tbsp soy sauce

½ large carrot, peeled and grated
1 cup cooked soybeans
2 tbsp sesame seeds, toasted

Rinse hijiki, and then place in a bowl with the water. While it soaks prepare the other ingredients.

Make the dressing by whisking together vinegar, sesame oil and soy sauce.

Toss carrots and soybeans with dressing in a medium-serving bowl.

Once hijiki has absorbed all the water, drain well and gently squeeze off any excess water. Add to salad.

Garnish with toasted sesame seeds. Serve cold.

FIESTA BEAN SALAD

As the name implies, this dish is finely suited to liven up any meal. Can't beat that in a salad!
Serves 6-8

- 3 cups black beans, cooked
- ½ medium red onion, diced
- ½ cup red bell pepper, diced
- 1 green onion, chopped
- 1 cup corn, fresh or frozen and cooked
- 1 tbsp each: ground cumin and Mexican seasoning
- 2 tsp garlic powder
- ½ cup lime juice
- pinch of cayenne pepper
- salt and pepper to taste

Combine ingredients in a medium serving bowl.

Mix and serve.

Arriba!

MIX BEAN SALAD

This colorful salad has a lovely tangy-sweet marinate. It is a versatile addition as a protein and fiber-rich side or try it over pasta, in wraps, or on green salad.
Serves 4-6

  2 cups garbanzo beans, cooked or canned and drained
  1 ½ cups kidney beans, cooked or canned and drained
  ¼ cup edamame, frozen or fresh and cooked
  ½ cup fresh green french beans, blanched
  ½ red bell pepper, thinly sliced

Marinade
  2 tbsp olive oil
  ½ tsp green curry paste
  ¼ cup apple cider vinegar
  ¼ cup raw sugar
  salt and pepper to taste
  2-4 tsp fresh cilantro, chopped

Mix first set of ingredients in a large serving bowl (garbanzo beans to bell pepper).

Prepare marinade. In a small bowl, whisk marinade ingredients until well combined.

Pour marinade over the salad. Mix gently. Chill and serve.

QUINOA SALAD

This is one of my favorites! It's so easy and so satisfying as a light meal or side dish.
Serves 8-10

- 2 cups quinoa
- 3 ½ cups water
- 1 medium beet, grated
- ½ cup green onion, chopped
- ½ cup red bell pepper, diced small
- ½ cup feta cheese, crumbled
- ¼ cup raisins (optional)
- 2 tbsp pine nuts
- ½ cup fresh parsley, chopped
- ½ cup fresh mint, chopped
- 2 tbsp olive oil
- ¼ cup apple cider vinegar
- salt and pepper to taste

Cook quinoa. Bring water to a boil in a medium pot. Add quinoa. Reduce heat, cover and simmer for 15 - 20 minutes or until water is absorbed. Remove from heat and let sit for 5 minutes. Fluff with a fork. Mix beet into quinoa while still hot. Let cool completely.

Toss together the beet, onion, bell pepper, feta cheese, raisins and pine nuts. Stir in cooled quinoa.

Add the parsley, mint, olive oil and vinegar. Salt and pepper to taste.

Chill for an hour or two before serving.

Vegan Option: Omit cheese

WARABI SALAD

Warabi is a baby fern and a bit of a Hilo specialty. Look for it at farmer's markets (also called "Ho'i'o" or fiddleheads). It grows wild so keep an eye out for it, especially in the spring.
Serves 4

- 1 bunch warabi
- ¼ medium red onion, sliced
- ¼ bell pepper, sliced
- 1 tsp ginger, peeled and thinly sliced
- 2 tsp sesame seeds
- 2 tsp rice vinegar
- 3 tbsp soy sauce

Fill a medium saucepan about half full of water and lightly salt. Bring to a boil.

Cut warabi into 1½- inch long pieces. Add to boiling water and blanch for 3 minutes. Rinse well with cold water to prevent warabi from turning brown.

Combine remaining ingredients in a large bowl. Add warabi. Stir to combine. Serve cold.

HEART OF PALM SALAD

This is a great recipe to hone your cutting skills. Practice making matchstick veggies with your julienne skills. As always, fresh is best, but in a pinch you can substitute 32 ounces of canned heart of palm.
Serves 6-8

- 2 lbs fresh heart of palm, sliced
- 1 medium red bell pepper, julienned
- 1 medium zucchini, julienned
- 1 bunch fresh cilantro, chopped coarsely
- ½ cup fresh lime juice
- ½ cup Sweet Chili Sauce (see page 18)
- 2 tbsp Bragg's amino acids
- 2 tbsp sesame oil
- 1 tbsp black sesame seeds

Prep vegetables and place in a medium bowl.

In a separate bowl, whisk together lime juice, chili sauce, Braggs and sesame oil. Pour over vegetables. Stir to combine.

Top with sesame seeds. Best if chilled before serving.

Raw Food Option: Use fresh heart of palm. Canned is not raw.

TABOULI

This Middle Eastern dish is easy to create and so very enjoyable. Day old tabouli is perfect for a healthy light lunch. For a change, try substituting a few ripe tomatoes for the bell pepper.
Serves 6-8

   4 cups water
   4 cups bulgur wheat
   ¾ cup lime juice
   ¾ cup olive oil
   1 large red bell pepper, diced
   2 cups green onion, chopped
   2 cups parsley, chopped
   1 cup mint, chopped
   1 tsp granulated garlic
   pinch white pepper
   pinch of cayenne
   salt to taste

In a medium saucepan, bring water to a boil. Remove from heat and stir in bulgur wheat. Cover and let stand for 30 minutes or until water is absorbed. Let cool.

Put the bulgur wheat in a large bowl. Add lime juice and olive oil. Lightly toss with the bell pepper, green onions, parsley, mint, garlic, pepper, cayenne and salt.

Refrigerate for a few hours before serving.

Gluten-Free Option: Substitute quinoa for the bulgur wheat.

Soups

Indian Potato Soup	V GF	55
Quinoa Soup	V GF	57
Vegan Corn Chowder	V	59
Roux 101		61
Vegan Ham & Bean Soup	V	62
Creamy Leek Soup	V GF	63
Vegan Potato Leek Soup	V	65
Miso Soup	V GF	66
Delightful Lima Bean Soup	V GF	67
Mushroom Barley Soup	V	69

INDIAN POTATO SOUP

Three cheers for the humble potato! Try this exciting variation of the simple classic potato soup. Adjust spice levels to your liking.
Serves 4-6

- 1 ½ tbsp safflower oil
- ½ large onion, chopped
- 1 clove garlic, chopped
- 1 tsp ground ginger
- 1 small leak, chopped
- 1 medium carrot, diced
- ¼ tsp each: cumin, garam masala, and curry powder
- 1 quart water
- 2 medium russet potatoes, cut into small chunks
- ¾ cups garbanzo beans, cooked and rinsed
- ¾ cups green peas
- 24 oz can diced tomato
- 2 tbsp fresh cilantro, chopped

In a large soup pot, sauté onion, garlic, ginger, leek and carrot in oil over medium heat for 10 minutes.

Add cumin, garam masala, and curry powder. Stir well. Add water and bring to a boil. Add potatoes and maintain a light boil for 20 minutes. Salt and pepper to taste.

Make sure potatoes are cooked. Add garbanzo beans, green peas, diced tomato and cilantro. Remove from heat. Stir well.

Cover for 10 minutes to let tastes meld.

Serve.

QUINOA SOUP

This soup fuels you with protein and vegetables. Seasonal vegetables, as always, can be substituted. Serves 6-8

- 1 cup quinoa
- 1 2/3 cup water
- 1 ½ tbsp safflower oil
- ½ large onion, chopped
- 2 clove garlic, chopped
- 2 tsp ground ginger
- 1 small (about 1 cup) leek, chopped
- 1 medium carrot, diced
- ½ tsp each: cumin, garam masala, and curry powder
- 1 quart water or stock
- 3 medium russet potatoes, cut into small chunks
- 1 cup (about 1 lb) zucchini, diced
- 14.5 oz can diced tomato
- dash of salt and pepper
- ¼ cup fresh cilantro, chopped

In a medium saucepan, prepare quinoa. Rinse quinoa. Bring water to a boil. Add quinoa. Cook partially covered at a low boil for 8-10 minutes until the water is just absorbed. Do not overcook or quinoa will loose its texture in the soup. Set aside.

In a large soup pot, sauté onion, garlic, ginger, leek and carrot in oil over medium heat, about 7-10 minutes until softening. Add cumin, garam masala, and curry powder. Stir well. Add water or stock and bring to a boil. Add potatoes and maintain a light boil, about 20 minutes or until potatoes are soft.

Add quinoa and diced tomatoes. Stir well. Remove from heat. Salt and pepper to taste.

Garnish with cilantro right before serving. Enjoy!

VEGAN CORN CHOWDER

This creamy, savory soup will satisfy your soul! Double the recipe for larger crowds or to ensure leftovers for lunch. Use organic corn to avoid GMO's in your diet!
Serves 4-6

  2 tbsp olive oil
  ½ rounded cup fakin bacon (vegan meat substitute)
  1 small yellow onion, diced
  1-2 medium carrots, diced
  3-4 stalks celery, diced
  1 ½ tsp basil
  1 ½ tsp oregano
  ½ tsp crushed red pepper flakes
  3 cloves garlic, crushed
  4 cups unchicken broth
  ½ cup water
  2 small russet potatoes, peeled and diced
  1 box (about 12 oz) silken soft tofu, pureed in blender
  2 cups sweet corn, fresh from the cob or frozen
  roux for thickening (see page 61)
  hickory salt and pepper to taste

  _____

In a large soup pot, sauté the fakin bacon in olive oil until crisp. Add onion, carrots, celery, basil, oregano and pepper flakes. Continue to sauté until onions are transparent. Add garlic and cook 2 minutes longer.

Add stock and potatoes. Bring to a boil over medium high heat. Turn heat down to maintain a low boil.

Once potatoes are soft, about 20 minutes, add roux to thicken. (Make sure to over-thicken a bit if using frozen corn, as it will thin it out.)

Add tofu and corn. Salt and pepper to taste.

Serve with a side salad and your favorite bread.

Roux 101

A roux is used to thicken soups or sauces. Additionally, a roux will lend a beautiful luster and body to the finished recipe.

It is quite easy to make a roux. Just remember, if you add too much liquid, slowly add more flour to balance your roux. You don't want a whole pot of paste!

Leave your ingredients handy, but start with:

¼ cup oil
½ cup flour
¼ cup broth or water

Heat the oil in a small saucepan over medium-low heat. Add the flour and whisk to incorporate. Turn the heat to low and, whisking the whole time, brown the roux until it turns tan or just brown, about 3 minutes. Do not to let it burn.

The longer you cook the roux, the nuttier and more intense the flavor.

Add the broth or water a little at a time. Whisk the liquid in to form a smooth batter-like consistency.

This is a handy technique to know. It will help improve the consistency of your soups.

VEGAN HAM & BEAN SOUP

Try this healthy, high fiber and high protein soup for a quick wholesome weekday meal. Substitute your favorite bean or a mix of beans.
Serves 6-8

1 tbsp olive oil
1 yellow onion, diced
2 tsp garlic
8 cups (½ gallon) water
½ cup nutritional yeast
1 tsp hickory salt
¼ cup white miso
roux to thicken (see page 61)
1 pack vegan ham, diced (we use Smart Deli)
3 cups pink beans, cooked and rinsed
salt and pepper to taste

In a large soup pot, sauté onions and garlic in olive oil over medium heat, about 10 minutes until onion is turning translucent. Add water, nutritional yeast and hickory salt. Bring to a light boil.

Reduce heat to simmer and add miso. Slowly add roux to thicken, stirring until combined to avoid clumping. Add vegan ham and beans.

Remove from heat. Salt and pepper. Serve.

CREAMY LEEK SOUP

This is a fabulous soup! Simple to make and simply enjoyable.
Serves 4-6

- 1 ½ tbsp olive oil
- ½ large onion, chopped
- 1 clove garlic, chopped
- 1 large or 2 small (about 1 lb.) leeks, chopped
- 1 medium carrot, diced
- 2 tbsp white wine
- 1 tsp Italian seasoning
- 1 - 2 cups water
- 3 medium (about 1 lb.) russet potatoes, cut into small chunks
- salt and pepper, to taste
- 1 cup soy milk
- ¾ cup corn, fresh or frozen
- 1 tbsp stone ground mustard
- 1 tbsp capers
- 1 tsp nutritional yeast
- 2 tbsp fresh parsley, chopped

In a large soup pot, sauté onion, garlic, leek and carrot in the olive oil over medium heat for 10 minutes. Add the white wine and Italian seasoning. Stir well.

Add 1 cup water and bring to a boil. Add potatoes and adjust with remaining water to cover. Maintain a light boil for 10- 15 minutes, until potatoes are soft. Salt and pepper to taste.

Once potatoes are cooked, reduce heat to low. (*See below.) Stir in soy milk, corn, mustard, capers, nutritional yeast and parsley. Stir well. Remove from heat. Cover for 10 minutes to rest.

Serve.

Tip: *For an even creamier soup, puree half of the soup in a food processor or blender. We recommend trying half first to preserve some of the variety of texture of the soup. However, you may prefer to blend all of the soup. Return to soup pot and continue.

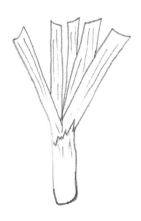

VEGAN POTATO LEEK SOUP

A variation of the Creamy Leek Soup. Creamy, dreamy and vegan to boot!
Serves 6-8

- 2 tbsp olive oil
- 2 leeks, cleaned and julienne
- 2 cloves garlic, crushed
- 3 quarts unchicken stock +
  ½ cup for roux
- 3 russet potatoes, diced
- ½ - 1 cup roux (see pg 61)
- ½ cup flour + more, as needed
- 1 ½ boxes (about 18 oz) soft silken tofu, whirled in a blender until smooth
- salt and pepper to taste

In a large soup pot, sauté leeks and garlic in olive oil over medium heat until soft, about 5 minutes. Add stock and potatoes. Bring to light boil. Boil until potatoes are soft, about 20 minutes. While potatoes boil, make a roux.

Once potatoes are soft, turn heat to simmer. Slowly add roux to thicken. Stir or whisk to avoid clumping.

Whirl tofu in a blender until smooth. Add blended tofu and stir to integrate into soup. Salt and pepper to taste. Turn off heat. Ring the dinner bell.

MISO SOUP

This soup is a delicious and simple Japanese staple. You can use either the mellower yellow miso paste or the stronger, saltier red miso paste. Experiment with vegetables of your choice.
Serves 4

- 4 cups water
- 4 whole shiitake mushroom
- 1 thumb-size piece of a ginger, thinly sliced
- 1 small round onion, sliced
- 1 medium Yukon gold potato, diced
- 3 tbsp miso paste
- ¼ cup wakame seaweed, crumbled
- 1 cup firm tofu, cut into cubes
- 1 green onion, chopped

Combine water, mushrooms, ginger, onion, and potato in a medium pot. Bring to a boil. Reduce heat to medium low and continue to boil until potatoes are tender, about 12 to 20 minutes.

Reduce heat to a simmer. Take out one cup of broth and mix with the miso paste in a small bowl. Stir well until paste is fully dissolved. Add this to the pot.

Keep soup at a simmer. Do not boil.

Add seaweed and tofu. Remove from heat. Garnish with the green onion.

Itadakimasu!

DELIGHTFUL LIMA BEAN SOUP

Lima beans are also known as butter beans. If these legumes are not a regular part of your healthy diet, make that switch right away as they have many health benefits. Look for fresh lima beans to truly delight your palate.
Serves 6-8

    1 lb dried lima beans, sorted and soaked overnight in the refrigerator
    ¼ cup olive oil
    1 clove garlic, minced
    2 tbsp shallot or round onion, minced
    5 large carrots, peeled and diced
    3 stalks celery, chopped
    1 leek, bulb only, chopped
    2 large tomatoes, diced
    1 tbsp curry powder
    2 cups vegetable stock
    6 cups + up to 2 cups water
    salt and pepper, to taste
    1 lb kale, chopped medium-sized and coarsely

Drain the soaked lima beans. Rinse the beans with clean water until the water runs clear. Set aside. (If using fresh beans, skip this step.)

In a large soup pot, heat the olive oil over medium high heat. Add the garlic and shallot. Sauté until caramelized.

Add the carrots, celery, leeks, tomatoes and lima beans. Stir for about 3 minutes to heat the vegetables up. Stir in curry powder.

Add the vegetable broth and water. Add 6 cups of water to start. Season with salt and pepper.

Simmer over low heat until lima beans are tender, 1 to 1½ hours. Stir occasionally. Add remaining water as needed to thin.

Once beans are cooked, stir in the kale. Cover for 2 to 3 minutes.

The soup is done. Serve piping hot.

MUSHROOM BARLEY SOUP

A hearty soup to warm you from the inside out. Try replacing pearled barley with whole grain hulled barley for a chewier and more nutritious soup.
Serves 6-8

    1 tbsp olive oil
    2 medium carrots, peeled and diced
    1 small round onion, diced
    1 small can (14.5 oz) diced tomatoes
    1 lb button mushrooms, sliced
    1 cup pearled barley
    8 cups water or vegetable stock
    salt and pepper to taste
    ½ cup fresh dill, chives or parsley leaves, minced

In a large soup pot, heat oil over medium heat. Add carrots, onion and tomato. Cook until soft, about 10 minutes. Add mushrooms and barley and cook 2 minutes more.

Add the broth and bring to a simmer. Reduce heat to low and partially cover pot. Soup should be bubbling, but only a little.

Simmer 15 to 20 minutes until barley is tender. Salt and pepper to taste. Stir in half of the fresh herbs. Remove from heat.

Serve in individual soup bowls topped with remaining herbs.

Soups on!

Tip: For hulled barley: Cook barley first. In a medium saucepan, bring 3 cups of water and 1 cup of hulled barley to a boil. Cover, reduce heat and simmer for 30-45 minutes, or until barley is soft. This can be done in advance. Add cooked barley after adding the broth. Reduce simmer time to 10 minutes.

Light Fare

Spring Rolls ∨ GF 72

Tofu Meatless Balls ∨ 73

Walnut Tofu Balls ∨ 74

Tofu Nuggets ∨ 75

Summer Rolls ∨ GF 77

Polenta Pizza ∨ GF 79

Eggplant Pockets ∨ GF 81

Seaweed Ahi Poke GF R 82

Mac Nut Ahi Poke GF R 82

Tofu Poke ∨ GF 83

Thai Tofu Salad ∨ GF 84

SPRING ROLLS

These lovely vegetable rolls are baked rather than fried. When folding, think of a tight little burrito closed at both ends. You'll get the knack.
Serves 6-8

1 package long rice
1 cup cilantro, chopped
15 oz straw mushrooms, chopped
8 oz can bamboo shoots, chopped
¼ cup + 1 tbsp soy sauce
2 tbsp Sweet Chili Sauce (see page 18)
2 tbsp sesame oil

1 package small rice spring roll wrappers
safflower oil for spraying

Soak long rice in enough hot water to cover for 5-10 minutes, per package directions. Strain.

In a medium bowl, add long rice and remaining ingredients together and mix well.

Prepare the wrappers by dipping them one sheet at a time into warm water. Lay on a towel to remove excess water before rolling. Divide filling evenly between wrappers. Fold and spray lightly with safflower oil.

Arrange on a baking sheet and cook for 15 minutes at 350 degrees F, until just browning.

Serve with our Sweet & Sour or Peanut Sauce.

TOFU MEATLESS BALLS

This is an enjoyable vegetarian "meat" ball. Try them alone with Sweet and Sour Sauce or add them to any pasta dish.
Serves 6-8

- 1 lb tofu, drained and crumbled
- 1 medium onion, diced
- 2 tsp vegetarian chicken seasoning
- 1 ½ cups nutritional yeast
- 1 ½ cups gluten flour
- 2 cups cooked brown rice

———————————————

Combine all ingredients in stand up mixer or large bowl. Mix until combined.

Use a spoon or small ice cream scoop to form balls about the size of a golf ball or as you wish.

Place on a cookie sheet. Bake at 350 degrees F for about 25 minutes or until firm.

WALNUT TOFU BALLS

This recipe is a variation of the Tofu Meatless Balls. They make a great appetizer or light entrée. Let the kids help scoop them and then gobble them up! Serves 6-8

- 1 lb tofu, drained
- 1 medium onion, chopped
- 1 tsp vegetarian chicken seasoning
- 2 tbsp brewers yeast
- 3 tbsp gluten flour
- 1 ½ cups cooked brown rice
- 2 cups walnut meal*

_____

Make sure tofu is well drained. Add all ingredients to a blender or food processor. Pulse to mix. Do not over mix.

Use an ice cream scoop to place balls on a cookie sheet.

Bake at 350 degrees F for 25 minutes or until golden brown.

*Walnut meal is nothing more than ground walnuts. You can easily make your own in a nut grinder, blender or food processor. Process slowly or you will make walnut butter. It should be gritty. Store in the freezer and use soon after making or buying.

TOFU NUGGETS

This is a versatile tofu preparation to add to your favorite sautéed mixed vegetables. These nuggets are also a delicious treat on their own.
Serves 6-8

　　3 lbs tofu, drained and cubed
　　½ cup teriyaki or black bean sauce
　　½ cup water
　　¾ cup flour

　　HOUSE SAUCE
　　½ cup Teriyaki Sauce (see page 19)
　　½ cup veganaise

　　1 medium onion, diced
　　1 medium zucchini, julienned
　　1 medium red bell pepper, diced
　　12 mushrooms, cut in half
　　1 tbsp olive oil, for sautéing

Place tofu in a large bowl.

In a separate bowl, whisk together the teriyaki or black bean sauce with the water. Pour this over the tofu and let sit for a few minutes until mostly absorbed.

Sprinkle flour over the tofu and gently stir to distribute.

Bake at 350 degrees F for 20 minutes, turning once, until golden brown crust forms. Let cool.

Meanwhile, make the House Sauce by whisking together the ingredients until smooth. Set aside.

Prepare the vegetables, or your favorite seasonal choices, by sautéing in oil until just tender, about 10 minutes.

In a medium serving bowl, add veggies and House Sauce to baked tofu nuggets.

Serve.

SUMMER ROLLS

Summer rolls make a wonderful light meal. The fresh ingredients leave your palate clean and your appetite satiated.
Serves 6

- ¼ package rice noodles
- 12 sheets rice paper rounds, (+ extras in case of tears)
- 12 pieces red leaf lettuce
- a handful fresh mint, divided
- 1 bunch fresh cilantro, divided
- 1 handful Thai basil leaves, divided
- 1 large carrot, shredded
- 1 medium cucumber, sliced thinly or julienned
- 1 bag alfalfa sprouts, divided
- use one or more of the following: teriyaki tofu, cut into 12 strips; avocado, cut into 12 thin strips; 6 jumbo shrimp, cut in half
- 1 ½ cup Peanut Sauce (see page 17)

Place rice noodles in a medium boil. Add enough boiling water to cover. Let stand until softened, about 15 minutes. Drain well. Set aside.

In a large bowl of warm water, soak rice paper rounds one at a time, until pliable, 30 seconds to 1 minute. Make sure there are no holes. Transfer to a flat surface.

Arrange 1 piece of lettuce on bottom half of each rice paper round. You may need to tear or fold the lettuce to fit. Leave a 1-inch border along bottom edge.

Top lettuce with mint, cilantro, basil, sprouts, carrot, cucumber, noodles and tofu, avocado or shrimp.

Roll up rice paper tightly around filling by folding in ends and continuing to roll.

Transfer summer roll to a plate. Serve with Peanut Sauce.

Tip: Amounts of herbs and veggies in each roll will vary with your personal preference.

POLENTA PIZZA

A wonderful appetizer or main dish, the toppings are totally adaptable to your tastes. Just think of the possibilities!
Serves 6-8 as appetizer or 4 as main dish

    olive oil, for pan
    3 cups water, or 2 ½ cups water and ½ cup milk of your choice
    ½ tbsp salt
    1 cup cornmeal
    2 cups Marinara Sauce (see page 14)
    ½ cup mushrooms, thinly sliced
    ¼ cup olives, sliced
    2-3 green onions, chopped
    1 cup block feta, crumbled
    ¾ cup each cheddar and mozzarella cheese
    ¼ cup Parmesan cheese

Brush oil on onto a baking sheet or pizza pan.

In a large saucepan, bring salted water to a boil. Add cornmeal, whisking to avoid lumps. Turn heat to low and simmer, whisking, then stirring, frequently until all the water is absorbed, 10 to 15 minutes.

Remove from heat and immediately spread polenta onto the baking sheet, about ½ inch thick.

Spread marinara sauce onto polenta base in the thickness you prefer. Scatter with mushroom, olives, green onion and feta somewhat evenly around the pizza. Top with remaining cheeses.

Bake at 350 degrees F for 20-30 minutes or until cheese is melted and crispy on top.

Tip: For a crispier polenta crust, spread polenta on cookie sheet and bake for 20 minutes or until crust begins to firm up and brown. Remove from oven. Proceed with adding sauce and toppings. Bake for an additional 10 minutes, or until cheese is melted and crispy.

Vegan Option: Use a dairy-free cheese alternative or simply omit cheese altogether.

EGGPLANT POCKET

These tasty little pockets are sure to satisfy. Great for lunch or dinner!
Serves 6-8

- 1 small onion, chopped
- 2 eggplants, baked and with skin removed, cubed
- 1 tsp garlic, chopped
- 1 tsp ground ginger (optional)
- 1 ½ tbsp safflower oil
- ¼ tsp each: cumin, garam masala, curry powder, paprika
- dash of salt and pepper
- 2 ¼ cup (about 1 lb) potatoes, cooked
- ¼ cup crushed tomato
- 1 bunch cilantro, chopped
- 1 cup green onion, sliced
- 1 package spring roll wrappers

Sauté the onion, eggplant, garlic and ginger in the oil over medium high heat, until softening, about 10 minutes. Add seasonings. Stir in potatoes and tomato. Remove from heat.

Divide the mix between the wrappers. Top each with cilantro and green onion. Fold wrappers in half. Press open edges closed.

Place on a baking sheet. Bake at 350 degrees F for 25-30 minutes, or until golden brown.

SEAWEED AHI POKE

A party wouldn't be a party without the poke. Use only the freshest, highest quality fish available. Serve as a light meal or pupu.
Serves 4-6

    2 lbs raw ahi, cut into cubes
    1 bunch (handful) ogo seaweed, chopped
    1 red onion, slivered
    1 cup green onion, chopped
    1-2 tsp chili pepper flakes
    3 tbsp soy sauce
    1 tsp sesame oil

Simply combine ingredients in a large bowl.

Chill. Serve.

MAC NUT AHI POKE

Add ½ cup chopped macadamia nuts to above ingredients.

Raw Food Option: Use raw macadamia nuts and raw soy sauce.

TOFU POKE

Tofu poke makes an outstanding appetizer. It is protein and mineral rich—and very delicious. Serves 8

3 lbs of tofu, well drained and cubed
½ cup (about a handful) ogo seaweed, coarsely chopped
1 red onion, slivered
1 cup green onion, chopped
1 cup soy sauce
½ cup sesame oil
¼ - 1 tbsp red chili pepper flakes, to taste
½ cup sesame seeds, toasted
1 tbsp Hawaiian salt

Put tofu in a medium serving bowl.

Rinse ogo seaweed in fresh water. Drain. Set aside.

Add remaining ingredients to tofu. Add seaweed. Stir to combine.

Chill for an hour or two before serving.

THAI TOFU SALAD

This is a long-time Island Naturals favorite. It's got a nice bite to it. It is wonderful in just about any circumstance—the beach, a potluck, family dinner. Make a batch and use it throughout the week for lunches.
Serves 6-8

3 lbs of firm tofu
1 cup green onion, chopped
1 cup fresh cilantro, chopped
½ cup soy sauce
2 tsp roasted sesame seeds
½ cup apple cider vinegar
3 tbsp sesame oil
generous 1-1 ½ cups Thai Tofu Dressing (next page)

Drain the tofu thoroughly to remove excess liquid. Cut tofu into bite-sized cubes.

Mix remaining ingredients in a serving bowl. Add tofu. Let stand while you make the Thai Tofu Dressing.

Let salad stand for a few hours before serving. Serve cold or at room temperature.

THAI TOFU SALAD DRESSING

Please adjust the spices to your liking. Try doubling it and keeping the extra for next time—or try drizzling it on soba noodles, in soup or over fish. Yields generous 1 ½ cup

- 2 tbsp ginger, minced
- 2 tbsp garlic, minced
- 1 cup safflower oil
- ¼ cup crushed red peppers
- ¼ cup hot paprika
- ½ tbsp sesame oil

You can mince the garlic and ginger in a food processor, if you prefer.

Place all ingredients in a jar. Shake well.

Keeps well in the refrigerator.

Ginger Lime Juice (pg 171)

Vegan Potato Leek Soup (pg 65)

Black & White Cupcakes (pgs 159 & 157)

Scones (pg 148)

Purple Sweet Potato Tapioca Pudding (pg 153)

Seaweed Salad (pg 46)

Thai Tofu Salad (pg 84)

Quinoa Salad (pg 50)

Spring Rolls with Sweet & Sour Sauce
(pgs 72 & 20)

Pesto (pg 16)

Sherry Chicken (pg 107)

Island Naturals Carrot Cake (pg 155)

Vegan Guacamole (pg 28)

Island Naturals Fry Rice (pg 140)

Lasagna (pg 124)

Chicken & Turkey Entrées

Chicken Enchiladas	GF	95
Coconut Chicken	GF	98
Tandoori Chicken	GF	100
Chicken Katsu		102
Indian Chicken Curry	GF	103
Thai Chicken Satay	GF	105
Sherry Chicken		107
Chicken Mole	GF	109
Turkey Meat Loaf	GF	110

CHICKEN ENCHILADAS

Agreeable and satisfying—a good enchilada is as much about confident improvising as it is about following a recipe. Use this as an introduction. Serves 4-6

- 2 lbs chicken, boneless and skinless thighs or breasts
- 1 tbsp paprika
- ½ tbsp garlic salt
- ½ tbsp cumin
- 1 tbsp chili powder
- salt & pepper to taste

- ¾ cup corn, fresh or frozen and cooked
- handful of fresh cilantro, stemmed and chopped

In a small bowl, mix spices together. Rub spice mixture on chicken.

Place chicken in an oven safe dish or on a cooking sheet. Bake at 350 degrees F for 30 minutes or until chicken is tender. Remove from oven and let cool.

Once cooled, thinly slice or pull off strips of the chicken. (You may also cut the chicken into bite-size cubes.) Put into a bowl and add corn and cilantro. Set aside.

BUILDING THE PIE

4 cups black or pinto beans, cooked or canned
2 cups (1 lb) cheddar cheese, shredded
1 cups (½ lb) jack cheese, shredded
1 recipe Ancho Chili Sauce (see page 12)
12 flour tortillas

In a 9 x 11 inch baking pan, place a layer of tortillas on bottom. Cover with thin layer of ancho chili sauce. Add a layer of beans. Add chicken. Top with one third of the cheeses. Repeat for a second layer. For final layer, put down tortillas, last of ancho chili sauce and cheese.

Bake covered at 350 degrees F for 10-15 minutes or until warm and bubbly. Remove cover and bake a final 10 minutes allowing cheese to brown lightly. Let stand for 5 minutes before serving.

Top with your favorites: guacamole, salsa, sour cream or plain yogurt, sliced olives, chilies, chopped cilantro, sunflower seeds...

Tip: Alternately, rather than enchilada pie style, you may roll up individual enchiladas. Simply cover the bottom of the pan with a thin layer of sauce. Warm the tortillas, for easy rolling, and cover both sides with sauce. This is easily done by pouring some sauce in a shallow pan or plate and dipping both sides. Divide the chicken and cheese filling between the tortillas. (Do not overfill or you might as well make the pie.) Roll them up and place them side-by-side in the baking dish and bake as above.

Gluten-Free Option: Use corn, teff or rice tortillas.

COCONUT CHICKEN

What's for dinner tonight? Why, coconut chicken, of course!
Serves 6-8

4 lbs chicken, skinless, boneless breasts or thighs

1 tsp green curry paste*
1 cup coconut milk + 1 can (14 oz)

1 red bell pepper, cubed
1 medium eggplant, cubed
2 medium zucchini, cubed
1 tbsp ginger, minced
2 sticks lemongrass, smash
½ cup Thai basil leaves
3 leaves kaffir lime
1/4 c cornstarch
1/4 c water
salt and pepper to taste

*We use Thai Kitchen Brand

Make curry sauce by combining curry paste mix with 1 cup coconut milk. (If you'd rather, you may substitute 1 cup prepared curry sauce of your choice.)

In an oven-safe baking dish, arrange chicken. Pour curry sauce in and marinate chicken for half an hour in the refrigerator.

Bake at 350 until done, about 25 to 30 minutes. Remove from oven, but keep warm.

While chicken cooks, in a medium saucepan sauté the ginger, lemongrass and vegetables in a little oil until tender over medium-high heat. Add remaining coconut milk and bring to a boil.

Combine cornstarch and water in a small bowl. Whisk until smooth. Add the cornstarch mix to the saucepan. Stir to avoid clumping.

Salt and pepper to taste.

Pour sauce over the baked chicken. Serve.

TANDOORI CHICKEN

Add this authentic Indian dish to your chicken entrée repertoire and you won't be sorry. It is easy to prepare, but needs to marinade for several hours, so plan ahead.
Serves 4-6

    4 lbs chicken, boneless and skinless breasts or thighs

MARINADE
- 2 tbsp ginger root, peeled and grated or crushed
- 2 tbsp garlic, minced
- 1 cup plain yogurt
- 2 tbsp sweet paprika
- 1 tbsp garam masala
- 2 tsp cardamom
- salt, to taste
- 1 tbsp cumin
- ¼ cup lime juice

- 1 cup onion, diced
- 2 cups carrot, sliced
- 2 cups peas, fresh or frozen

Arrange chicken in a deep baking dish.

In a medium bowl, mix all marinade ingredients together. Whisk to combine. Pour over chicken and marinade for 4-8 hours in the refrigerator.

When ready to prepare, bake chicken at 350 degrees F until tender, about 30 minutes.

While chicken cooks, sauté onion and carrot over medium high heat until tender, about 10 minutes. Add peas and sauté for about 2 more minutes.

Add vegetables to cooked chicken and serve.

CHICKEN KATSU

This version of Japanese fried chicken is baked rather than fried in the interest of health. Serve with tonkatsu sauce or barbeque sauce over shredded cabbage or two scoops of rice.
Serves 4-6

- 4 lbs chicken, skinless, boneless breasts or thighs
- 2 eggs
- splash of half & half
- 1 ½ cup panko (Japanese bread crumbs)
- 2 tbsp paprika
- salt and pepper to taste

Rinse chicken and drain thoroughly. Set aside.

Whisk together the eggs and half & half.

In a medium bowl, combine panko, paprika, salt and pepper. Set aside.

Dip each piece of chicken in the egg mixture then coat with the panko mixture.

Lay breaded chicken pieces on a baking sheet. Bake at 350 degrees F for 30 minutes or until golden brown.

INDIAN CURRY CHICKEN

You'll need to start this dish the night before to let it marinade. From there, it is quite quick and easy to prepare for a pleasingly rich meal.
Serves 4-6

    4 lbs chicken, skinless, boneless breasts or thighs, cut into bite-sized pieces

MARINADE
    1 tbsp garlic, minced
    1 tbsp ginger, minced
    ½ cup plain yogurt
    ½ tbsp each: curry, garam masala, turmeric
    ½ tbsp salt and pepper

    1 tbsp olive oil, for sautéing
    1 clove garlic, minced
    4 medium potatoes, peeled and cubed
    1 large carrot, peeled and diced
    2 tbsp fresh cilantro or green onion, chopped, for garnish

---

Prepare marinade by whisking ingredients until combined. Add to chicken and marinade overnight in the refrigerator.

When ready to prepare dish, heat oil in a large skillet or wok over medium high heat, add garlic, potatoes and carrot. Sauté for about 10 minutes until potatoes begin to cook through.

Add marinated chicken with any remaining marinade. Cover and cook, stirring occasionally. Continue to sauté until chicken is cooked, about 15 minutes. Add a bit of water if it becomes too dry during this cooking time.

Arrange on individual plates and garnish with green onion.

THAI CHICKEN SATAY

This will be a favorite for the whole family! It marinades overnight, so plan ahead. (Though in a pinch you can shorten or lengthen the marinating time.) You will also need to have 8-inch skewers on hand. Serve this succulent dish with Peanut Sauce. Serves 4-6

2 lbs chicken, boneless and skinless breasts or thighs

1 tsp curry powder
½ tsp turmeric powder
1 tsp garlic, minced
½ tsp cumin
1 tbsp paprika powder
¼ cup coconut milk
3 tbsp Sweet Chili Sauce (see page 18)
½ tsp salt
1 tbsp soy sauce
1 tbsp sesame oil

1 recipe Peanut Sauce (see page 17)

Cut chicken into long strips, approximately 1 ½ inches thick.

Add remaining ingredients in a large bowl. Add chicken strips, cover and let marinade overnight in the refrigerator.

When ready to prepare, thread 3 pieces of marinated chicken onto each skewer. Leave the bottom quarter of the skewer as a handle.

Bake at 350 degrees F, about 30 minutes, depending on the thickness of the chicken. Alternately, grill on barbeque for 10-15 minutes. In both cases, turn skewers once during cooking.

Enjoy with our Peanut Sauce, vegetable kabobs and rice.

SHERRY CHICKEN

This is an elegant dish with hints of sherry. It provides a sophisticated outcome for minimal effort.
Serves 6-8

- 4 lbs of chicken, boneless and skinless breasts or thighs
- 4 tbsp olive oil, divided half for baking chicken and half for sautéing

SAUCE
- ½ cup flour + ½ cup olive oil, for roux
- ½ medium onion, sliced
- 2 ½ cups whole milk
- salt and pepper to taste
- 2 tbsp pizza seasoning
- 3-4 tbsp chicken broth powder
- ½ cup sherry

- 1 bell pepper, julienned
- 2 cups mushrooms, sliced in half
- 1 medium zucchini, julienned

First prepare the chicken by arranging it in a lightly oiled casserole dish. (You will later add vegetables and sauce to this cooking dish so make sure it is deep enough.) Brush chicken with olive oil and lightly salt and pepper.

Bake chicken at 350 degrees F for about 30 minutes, or until chicken is thoroughly cooked. Reserve any chicken grease from baking pan in a separate bowl.

Now prepare the sherry sauce. Make the roux by whisking the flour and oil together. Set aside.

In a medium saucepan, heat olive oil over medium high heat. Add onion and sauté until golden brown. Reduce temperature to medium-low and add milk. Stir constantly. Add saved chicken grease. Add salt and pepper, pizza seasoning and chicken broth powder. Continue stirring. Bring mixture to just before boiling, continuing to stir.

Add roux slowly, stirring to avoid clumping. Add sherry. Continue to simmer for a few minutes. Remove from heat. Cover.

Prepare vegetables to your liking—we suggest sautéing the bell pepper, mushrooms and zucchini over medium high heat or lightly steaming them.

Add cooked veggies to the chicken in the casserole dish. Pour the sauce over the dish. Cover to keep warm until you are ready to serve.

CHICKEN MOLE

This is a rich and impressive dish. Cooking the chicken directly in the mole sauce ensures it will be tender and flavorful.
Serves 4-6

- 4 lbs chicken, skinless and boneless thighs or breasts

- ½ ancho chili
- ½ chipotle pepper
- ½ cup cacao powder
- 2 tbsp cilantro roots
- ¼ medium yellow onion, cut into chunks
- 1 ½ tbsp garlic
- 3 tbsp tomato paste
- 1 bell pepper, cut into chunks
- 1 ½ cups (12 oz) pureed tomato, fresh or canned

_____

Place chicken in a deep baking dish.

Mix remaining ingredients in a blender. Blend on high until it becomes a well-combined sauce. Pour sauce over chicken.

Bake covered at 350 degrees F, about 30 minutes, until chicken is tender.

Tip: Reserve cilantro leaves and use as a garnish.

TURKEY MEAT LOAF

Here's a wonderful adaptation of this comfort food. Use leftovers, if there are any, for cold sandwiches. Serves 4-6

- 2 lbs ground turkey
- 1 medium carrot, chopped
- 1 large onion, chopped
- 2 medium stalks celery, chopped
- 1 bunch fresh parsley
- ¾ cup veganaise
- 1 cup instant mashed potatoes
- 2 tsp Spike seasoning
- 1 tsp salt and pepper, to taste

Place turkey in a large bowl.

Put carrot, onion, celery and parsley in a food processor and pulse until minced. Do not puree.

Add minced vegetables and remaining ingredients to turkey. Mix well until evenly distributed. Go ahead and use your hands for this.

In a lightly oiled 9 by 13 inch pan, form into a 9 by 5 inch oval loaf. Alternately, press into a loaf pan. Bake at 350 degrees F for 1 hour, until thoroughly cooked.

Fish Entrées

Island Naturals Alaskan Salmon — GF — 112

Fish Stew — 113

Stuffed Bell Peppers — 115

Salmon Croquettes — 117

Island Naturals Lau Lau — GF — 119

ISLAND NATURALS ALASKAN SALMON

We recommend wild Alaskan salmon for this dish. The outcome is delicate yet dramatic and is sure to satisfy.
Serves 2

- 2 fillet of Alaskan salmon, bones and skin removed
- 1 tsp olive oil, for baking dish
- 1 tbsp sea salt
- 1 medium red onion, thinly sliced
- 3 small limes, sliced into thin circles
- ½ - 1 ½ cups mayonnaise
- 2 cups Teriyaki Sauce (see page 19)

Arrange fillets in a lightly oiled baking dish. Salt the salmon fillets. Cover fillet with a ¼ to ½ inch layer of mayonnaise (I know it sounds like a lot, but trust me). Top the fillets with onion and lime slices. Drizzle about half the teriyaki sauce over the whole dish.

Bake at 400 degrees F for 10-20 minutes. The dish is done when the mayonnaise and limes are golden and when fish is easily flaked with a fork.

Remove from oven and drizzle with remaining teriyaki sauce.

FISH STEW

This stew comes together beautifully with its combination of fish, aromatic seasoning and vegetables. It is topped with mashed potatoes to fully bring it into the comfort food realm.
Serves 4-6

- 2 tbsp safflower oil, divided
- ½ medium onion, diced
- ½ tsp garlic, minced
- 1 tsp ginger, minced
- 1 tsp cumin powder
- ½ tsp coriander powder
- 2 tbsp flour
- 2 cups water, more as needed to maintain desired thickness
- 1 tbsp unchicken broth
- 1 cup diced tomato
- 2 tbsp tomato paste

- 1 lb fish (we recommend white fish of your choice), cut into small pieces
- ½ cup cauliflower, cut into flowerets
- ½ cup spinach, chopped
- 2 cup mashed potatoes
- ¼ cup fresh parsley, chopped

Begin by preparing the broth. Heat 1 tbsp of the oil in a medium pan over medium high heat. Add onion, garlic, ginger, cumin, and coriander. Sauté until onion becomes transparent, about 10 minutes.

Slowly add flour, stirring constantly for about 2 minutes. Slowly add water and broth, stirring constantly to avoid clumping of the flour. Turn heat down to medium low. Bring to a light boil and stir until it begins to thicken into a sauce. Stir in diced tomatoes and tomato paste. Remove from heat. Set broth aside.

In a large frying pan, add remaining oil and heat over medium high heat. Sauté fish and cauliflower until fish is just cooked, about 5-7 minutes (time will vary depending on type of fish).

Add 2 cups of broth and spinach. Bring to a simmer. Add remaining broth. You want the fish stew to be a bit thinner than you like your final stew. You may add water if it is too thick.

Remove from heat and pour into a baking dish. Place mashed pot on top, as evenly as possible.

Bake at 350 degrees F until potatoes are golden brown, about 20 minutes.

Garnish with chopped parsley.

STUFFED BELL PEPPERS

A filling, healthy main dish. Serving size is one bell pepper (two halves) per person—adjust recipe accordingly to feed two or twenty.
Serves 6

- 6 large green bell peppers
- 2 tbsp olive oil, plus more for brushing peppers
- 3 cups whole grain bread, diced
- 2 tsp Spike seasoning
- 1 medium onion, diced
- 1 cup leeks, thinly sliced
- ½ lb cooked salmon, flaked
- ½ cup veganaise
- 1 cup jack cheese, shredded

Cut peppers in half and remove seeds. Brush the peppers with olive oil. Set them in a shallow baking dish and bake at 350 degrees F for about 5 minutes. (Leave oven on.) Do not over bake peppers—this step is simply to soften them.

Combine bread and Spike together in a medium bowl. Set aside.

Heat the oil in a wok or frying pan. Stir-fry the onion and leeks over medium high heat until translucent, about 5 minutes. Add to bread bowl. Add remaining ingredients and stir gently to combine.

Divide filling into peppers. Top with cheese. Return peppers to the baking dish. Bake at 350 degrees F for 20-30 minutes, until peppers are tender.

So rewarding!

SALMON CROQUETTES

A simple and pleasing dinner—especially easy if you have leftover potatoes or fish. Baked rather than fried to preserve your good health and its good taste.
Serves 6-8

1 lb salmon
2 lbs potatoes, peeled and diced
1 round onion, minced
½ cup green onion or leeks, thinly cut
1 ½ cups panko (Japanese bread crumbs)

SAUCE
4 oz sour cream
¼ cup fresh dill, minced
¼ cup half and half
salt and pepper, to taste

Put salmon in a baking dish. Add enough water to cover the salmon. Cover and bake at 350 degrees F until done, about 15 - 20 minutes. Remove from oven and let cool. Once cooled, pull salmon into small pieces.

Meanwhile, add peeled potatoes to a pot of boiling water. Reduce heat to maintain low boil until potatoes are cooked, about 10 minutes. Strain.

While potatoes boil and salmon cooks, sauté the onion and green onion or leeks until golden brown. Remove from heat.

Now that everything is prepped, combine fish, potatoes, veggies and panko in a food processor. Pulse until combined. Do not over process; you want lots of texture and recognizable ingredients. (You may use a potato masher instead.)

Use your hands to form 2-3 inch round patties. Place on an oiled baking sheet. Bake at 350 degrees F until golden brown, about 20 minutes.

While baking, make sauce by combining all ingredients and whisking or blending until well combined.

Spoon sauce over warm croquettes and serve.

ISLAND NATURALS LAU LAU

This favorite traditional Hawaiian dish is fabulous. Plan ahead to allow for cook time. Better make double for your next luau or potluck!
Makes 4 lau lau

16 taro leaves
2 quarts water
4 tsp Hawaiian salt, divided

4 chicken thighs or 2 chicken breasts, boneless and skinless, cut into pieces
½ lb ahi fish, cut into pieces
½ lb yams or taro root, chopped

Fill a large pot about ¾ full of water. Bring water to a boil. Add 2 tsp of salt and the taro leaves. Boil for 20 minutes. Pull leaves out with tongs and keep water.

Pat leaves dry. Lay 4 taro leaves together to form each lau lau. In the center of the leaves, add a piece of chicken, fish, yam and ½ teaspoon of salt.

Fold up the leaves (much like you would a square burrito.) Wrap tightly in foil.

Return wrapped lau lau to the pot of water and bring to a boil on medium low heat. Partially cover with lid. Maintain a low boil for approximately 4 hours. Add more water as necessary to keep water level above lau lau.

Lau lau is done when leaves are soft. Remove with tongs and let cool a bit. Discard foil and serve.

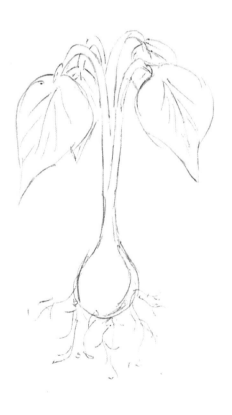

Vegetarian Entrées

Eggplant Parmesan   GF   122

Lasagna   GF   124

Savory Tofu   126

Moroccan Stew   V GF   128

Calzones   130

Goma-Dare Tofu   V GF   132

Pad Thai   V GF   133

EGGPLANT PARMESAN

The trick to a perfect outcome is to let the eggplant dry completely before cooking. Use the freshest eggplant possible.
Serves 6-8

---

2 medium round eggplants
1 ½ tsp salt (for salt water)
1 tsp Italian seasoning
¼ cup olive oil
1 cup half & half
½ cup fontinella cheese, grated
1 ½ c Marinara Sauce, warmed (see page 14)
1 cup mozzarella cheese, grated
2 tbsp Parmesan cheese, grated
Salt & pepper to taste

Cut eggplant into ½ inch thick rounds.

Soak in salted water just enough to cover eggplant for 10 minutes. Remove and let drain in a colander. Place eggplant on a towel and pat dry with a second towel to remove excess water. Arrange eggplant on a baking sheet.

In a small bowl, combine Italian seasoning and olive oil. Drizzle over eggplant.

Bake at 350 degrees F for 15 minutes, until golden brown. Remove from pan and set aside to cool.

While eggplant cools, in a medium saucepan, combine half & half and grated fontinella cheese. Heat over medium low heat until combined to form a thick sauce. Stay close and stir frequently.

Cover the bottom of a casserole pan with marinara sauce. Add a layer of eggplant. Cover with remaining marinara sauce. Next drizzle cheese sauce. Then top with mozzarella cheese. Sprinkle Parmesan cheese over top.

Return to oven and bake at 350 degrees F for about 30 minutes, until cheese is melted and sauce is bubbly. Allow to rest for 10 minutes before serving.

Serve with your best green salad and warmed garlic bread.

LASAGNA

This signature dish is served everyday at each Island Naturals location—it is that popular. So uncork that red wine, slice some rustic bread and indulge!
Serves 6-8

- 2 lb raw (2 cup cooked) spinach, excess water drained
- 3 cups Marinara Sauce (see page 14)
- 1 recipe homemade or 1 package lasagna, cooked al dente
- 1 cup zucchini, sliced
- 2 cups ricotta cheese
- 2 cups jack cheese
- ½ cup mozzarella cheese
- ¼ cup Parmesan cheese

In a large saucepan, blanch or steam spinach until just wilted. The spinach should retain its vibrant color.

Layer ingredients directly into 8 x 11 inch baking pan in the following order: sauce to cover the bottom of the pan, then a single layer of lasagna noodles. Top with sauce, zucchini, ricotta cheese and jack cheese. Next add a second layer of noodles, sauce, spinach, ricotta cheese and jack cheese. The final layer is as follows: lasagna noodles, sauce, and mozzarella cheese. Sprinkle Parmesan cheese over top.

Bake covered at 350 degrees F for 30-40 minutes. Uncover and bake another 10 minutes or until top is slightly browned.

Bellissima!

Tip: Leftover lasagna freezes well. Cut into single serving size before freezing for a delicious and nutritious lunch box meal.

Gluten-Free Option: Use gluten-free lasagna noodles.

SAVORY TOFU

This dish will make a tofu lover out of anyone! Be sure to really drain the tofu well. You can then let it marinade as time allows—overnight or ten minutes.
Serves 6-8

4 cups (2 lbs) tofu, drained well and cut into ¾ inch cubes
1 tbsp garlic, minced
salt and pepper to taste
1 cup safflower oil + more for wok

SAUCE
1 medium onion, sliced
1 cup soy sauce or Braggs
½ cup white wine
¾ cup lime juice
2 tbsp cornstarch
1 tbsp water

2 cups kale, coarsely chopped
1 cup bean sprouts
½ bunch of cilantro, chopped
½ bunch green onion, chopped

Place tofu in a large bowl. Mix garlic, pepper, salt, and oil in a small bowl. Add to tofu and mix gently. Let marinade stand for at least 10 minutes.

Place tofu on rimmed baking sheets. Bake at 350 degrees F until lightly puffed, about 20 minutes. Remove from oven.

Meanwhile, prepare the sauce. In a medium pan, sauté the onion in oil over medium high heat until it caramelizes, about 5 minutes.

Add soy sauce, white wine and lime juice. Bring to a boil.

Combine cornstarch with water and whisk until smooth. Stirring constantly, slowly add to sauce. Turn off heat. Let stand. Sauce will thicken as it cools. (If sauce does not thicken enough, add more cornstarch mixture a bit at a time.)

Coat a wok with a bit of oil on medium high heat. Add tofu and sauce. Stir to combine. Add kale. Stir to distribute very briefly, just until kale wilts slightly, and remove from heat. Garnish with bean sprouts, cilantro and green onion.

Serve.

MOROCCAN STEW

You will go wild for the complex flavor of this aromatic stew. The warming spices alone will transport you to another time and place. Don't be scared off by the long ingredients list—this stew is amazingly quick and simple.
Serves 4-6

1 cup safflower oil
2 tbsp paprika
1 tbsp turmeric
1 tbsp curry powder
1 tbsp mustard seeds
1 tbsp cumin seeds
2 tsp cumin powder
2 tsp cinnamon
¾ tsp cayenne powder

1 - 2 medium cloves garlic, minced
½ medium onion, diced
1 cup carrots, sliced
1 cup sweet yam, cubed
1 cup potato, cubed
1 cup zucchini, sliced
1 cup eggplant, cubed
½ medium red bell pepper, diced

1 - 2 cups water or broth, to desired thickness
2 cups garbanzo beans, cooked or canned and drained

½ cup raisins, optional
salt and pepper to taste

In a medium soup pot, heat the oil over medium heat. Add all spices and sauté for 2 minutes, stirring occasionally, until spices are aromatic. Turn heat down to medium low.

Add garlic and onion. Sauté until onion is soft and translucent, about 5 minutes. Add remaining vegetables and stir to coat. Continue to cook until just tender, about 2-5 minutes. Salt and pepper to taste.

Add 1 cup water or broth to start. Add garbanzo beans and raisins. Bring to a boil, stirring occasionally. Reduce heat to low. Cover and simmer until potatoes and yams easily split with a fork, about 20 minutes. If stew is too thick, add more water or broth slowly to desired consistency.

Adjust salt and pepper.
Serve.

CALZONES

Pizza in a pocket! This is a highly adaptable recipe, so go ahead and substitute your favorite pizza toppings. Our Pesto works great with or in place of the Marinara Sauce too.
Makes 6 calzones

2 ½ cups flour + more for rolling and dusting
1 ½ tsp yeast
1 ½ tsp salt
1 tsp Italian seasoning
1 tbsp sugar
1 cup warm water
3 tbsp olive oil, divided + more for brushing

1 onion, diced
1 medium zucchini, diced
1 medium red bell pepper, diced
3 cloves of garlic, minced
1 cup olives, sliced
2 cups Marinara Sauce (see page 14)
2 lbs jack cheese, grated
¼ cup Parmesan cheese, grated

First make your crust. In a large bowl, mix flour, yeast, salt, Italian seasoning and sugar. Make a well in the center and add water and 2 tbsp olive oil. Gently mix by hand or in a stand up mixer until you form a dough ball. If it is too sticky, add a little bit of flour at a time.

Leave the ball of dough in the bowl and set aside. Let dough rise to double its size.

Meanwhile, prepare the filling. Heat 1 tbsp oil in a medium frying pan. Sauté the onion, zucchini, bell pepper and garlic over medium high heat, until beginning to soften, about 5 minutes. Remove from heat and stir in olives. Set aside.

Once dough has doubled in size, punch it down. Divide dough into 6 equal pieces. Dust your work area with flour and roll each piece into a 6-inch circle.

Divide the filling evenly between the dough pieces. Place 1/6 of the filling, marinara sauce and cheese onto one side of each dough circle. Pull the other half over the filling to create your calzone. Pinch along the seam to seal dough.

Brush the top of each calzone with oil and sprinkle with a few pinches of Parmesan cheese.

Bake at 350 degrees F for 25 minutes, or until crust is lightly browned and filling is hot.

Serve with a side of your favorite dressing or more marinara sauce.

GOMA-DARE TOFU

Goma-dare is an amazing Japanese sesame sauce used for dipping or cooking. Serve this dish with brown rice.
Serves 6-8

3 lbs tofu, drained and cubed

1 cup sesame seeds
¼ cup brown sugar
2 tbsp mirin
2 tbsp soy sauce

1 cup cut green beans
1 cup assorted mushrooms

Bake cubed tofu at 350 degrees F for 15-20 minutes on an oiled cookie sheet until lightly puffed and browned.

While tofu bakes, prepare sauce. Dry roast sesame seeds. Set aside ¼ cup of seeds in a small bowl. In a grinder or with a mortar and pestle, grind remaining ¾ cup sesame seeds until powdery. Combine with whole seeds. Stir in brown sugar, mirin and soy sauce.

Over medium high heat, sauté the green beans and mushrooms in the sauce until crisp tender, about 8 minutes. Add tofu for final few minutes.

PAD THAI

It is the tamarind that gives this dish its authentic orange hue and sweet flavor. You may add up to 3 cups of baked or sautéed tofu, chicken or shrimp. Serves 6-8

16 oz rice noodles

SAUCE

4 tbsp safflower oil, divided

2 cloves garlic, minced

½ medium yellow onion, thinly sliced

2 tbsp paprika

2 tbsp ketchup

2 tsp sugar

1 tbsp soy sauce

2 tbsp distilled vinegar

¼ cup tamarind paste

VEGETABLES

½ medium onion, thinly sliced

½ cup carrots, julienned

½ cup broccoli, trimmed to bite-size

2 cup Napa cabbage, shredded

¼ cup cilantro, chopped

1 handful mung bean sprouts

1-2 green onions, chopped

1 tbsp peanuts, roasted and crushed (optional)

Soak rice noodles in cold water until they soften. Drain. Bring 6 cups of water to a boil, add rice noodles. Cook until halfway done* (per package instructions). Drain under cold running water. Set aside.

Prepare the pad thai sauce. Heat 2 tbsp oil in a medium saucepan over medium high heat. Sauté the garlic, onion, paprika, ketchup and sugar for 2 minutes. Stir in soy sauce and vinegar. Bring to a boil. Whisk in the tamarind paste, being sure it breaks up completely. Turn off heat. Set aside.

Now prepare the vegetables. In a large frying pan, sauté onion, carrot, broccoli, cabbage and cilantro with remaining oil, over medium heat until tender. Add in sauce and bring to a simmer. Turn off heat.

Add noodles and toss gently until everything is covered in the sauce. Garnish with sprouts, green onions and peanuts.

Enjoy!

Tip: *For pad thai, you will undercook the noodles a bit as they will continue to cook when stir-frying. If your noodles are perfectly cooked, they are too soft for pad thai and will ensure a mushy stir-fry. Think of the Thai equivalent to al dente!

Side Dishes

Garlic Rosemary Roasted
  Potatoes   V GF   136
Asian Rice Pilaf   V GF   137
Preparing Basmati Rice   138
Island Naturals Fry Rice V GF 140
Mexican Rice   V GF   142
Thai Curry Rice   V GF   143

GARLIC ROSEMARY ROASTED POTATOES

This fragrant dish can be made using your favorite variety of potatoes. We suggest red, Yukon gold, new potatoes or russet.
Serves 4-6

- 4 lbs potatoes, cubed
- ¼ cup olive oil
- 1 tbsp garlic, fresh or granulated
- 1 tbsp fresh rosemary, minced
- ½ tbsp salt
- ¼ tbsp white pepper

Wash potatoes well. You can peel them, if you prefer.

In a large bowl, whisk together olive oil, garlic, rosemary, salt and pepper. Toss in the potatoes, stirring gently to distribute evenly.

Spread potatoes on an ungreased baking sheet.

Bake at 425 degrees F until golden on the outside and soft in the middle, approximately 20 - 30 minutes, turning occasionally.

Serve warm with your favorite chicken, fish or tofu dish.

ASIAN RICE PILAF

The beautifully aromatic basmati rice is grown in India and Pakistan. It adds a special delicacy to this pilaf. Reward your senses with this lovely dish. Serves 4-6

1 cup basmati rice

¼ cup sesame oil
¼ cup safflower oil
1 tsp fresh ginger, minced
½ small yellow onion, diced
¾ cup carrots, diced
1 small bell peppers, diced
1 stalk celery, thinly sliced
¾ cup green peas
¼ cup Braggs
1 cup green onion, chopped

Prepare the basmati rice; see page 138.

Heat the oil in a wok or large frying pan and stir-fry the ginger and onion. Add vegetables and cook until tender, about 10 minutes. Remove from heat and add Braggs.

Combine rice and stir fried veggies. Garnish with green onion.

PREPARING BASMATI RICE

Don't get too hung on the rice prep. Trust your inner cook!

1 cup dry rice yields about 3 cups cooked rice.

Step 1: Rinse the rice.
Rinse the rice two or three times in fresh water. Run your hand through the rice. This will remove excess starch.

Step 2: Soak the rice.
Soak in a bowl of cold water for 15 minutes to 1 hour. Longer soaking time adds more moisture to the grains thus reducing cook time and makes for plump individual grains. Drain the water once it is milky—you will need to change the water 2 or 3 times.

Step 3: Cook the rice.
Bring water to a boil over high heat. Add rice and salt. Stir. Return water to a boil. Reduce heat to simmer. Cover. Set a timer. Cook white basmati rice about 11 minutes. Cook brown about 25 minutes. It is done when you no longer hear the water bubbling. Don't peek during cooking unless totally necessary.

The amount of water required for 1 cup of rice will vary according to how long the rice was soaked. Use less water if you want a firm grain, more for a tender grain. General ratio is 1:2, rice to water.

Step 4: Rest the rice.
When timer goes off, turn heat off. Let rice sit for 10 minutes without removing the lid.

Step 5: Fluff and enjoy!
Fluff with a fork. Serve warm.

ISLAND NATURALS FRY RICE

For an even easier method, pan fry leftover cooked rice with a bit of sesame oil before adding to the tofu and vegetables. Delicious!
Serves 4-6

1 cup brown or basmati rice
2 ½ cups water

1- 2 tbsp safflower oil, divided
½ stalk celery, diced
1 medium carrot, diced
½ yellow onion, diced
2 cloves garlic, chopped
1 tbsp ginger, chopped
¼ cup peas, fresh or frozen
2 tbsp sesame oil

1 cup firm tofu, drained well and crumbled
¼ cup Braggs or low-sodium soy sauce
½ tsp turmeric

¼ cup soy sauce
3 tbsp sesame oil

½ cup green onion, diced
5-10 strips of fakin' bacon, baked and crumbled (optional)

For brown rice, combine rice and water. Bring to a boil. Cover and lower heat to simmer 30 minutes or until water is absorbed. Basmati rice directions are on page 138.

Sauté celery, carrot, onion, garlic and ginger in 1 tbsp of oil over medium high heat until crisp tender. Add peas for last minute or so of sauté. Remove from heat.

In a bowl, combine crumbled tofu with turmeric and Braggs. Bake tofu on a rimmed baking dish for 10 minutes at 350 degrees F. Alternately, sauté tofu in remaining oil until outside browns.

In a medium serving bowl, add cooked rice, soy sauce and sesame oil. Mix to coat. Add tofu and veggies. Stir to combine.

Garnish with green onion and fakin' bacon.

Tip: The fakin' bacon adds a nice smoky taste to the dish.

MEXICAN RICE

This is a wonderful side dish for any Mexican meal.
Serves 4-6

- 2 cups white long grain rice
- ½ cup safflower oil
- 4 cups water

- 1 tsp garlic, minced
- 1 jalapeño pepper, diced
- 1 scant cup (7 oz) tomato puree
- 1 tsp paprika
- 1 medium tomato, chopped
- 1 bunch cilantro including the roots, coarsely chopped
- ¼ round onion, cut in chunks

- ½ tbsp safflower oil
- 1 bell pepper, diced
- 1 onion, diced
- 1 cup corn, frozen or fresh and cooked
- salt and pepper to taste
- ¼ cup cilantro, chopped

In a medium saucepan, pan fry rice in oil over medium heat for 3-5 minutes. Add water and cook rice. (Bring to a boil, reduce heat to simmer, cover and cook 15 minutes or until water is absorbed.)

Place garlic, jalapeño, tomato puree and paprika in a blender and puree.

Place tomato, cilantro and onion in a large serving bowl. Add puree. Stir in rice.

Sauté the bell pepper and diced onion in oil until tender, about 10 minutes. Add corn for last two minutes. Salt and pepper to taste.

Top the rice with the sautéed vegetables and garnish with remaining cilantro.

THAI CURRY RICE

This dish will have everyone following their nose to the kitchen table. Try it with Coconut Chicken (pg 98).
Serves 4-6

3 cups basmati rice, cooked (see page 138)

½ cup cilantro, coarsely chopped, divided
1 small onion, chunked
thumb size piece of ginger, chopped
2-3 cloves garlic, coarsely chopped
3 kaffir lime leaves
3 Thai basil leaves
3 tbsp soy sauce
3 tbsp lime juice

1 cup coconut milk, divided
1½ tsp curry powder
1½ tsp turmeric

1 red bell pepper, diced
1 cup soybeans, cooked
Salt and pepper

———————————————

Set aside a third of the cilantro to use as garnish later.

In a blender, add first set of ingredients (from cilantro to lime juice). Add enough coconut milk to cover. Blend until smooth. Set aside.

In a skillet, pan-fry the curry powder & turmeric together over medium high heat until aromatic, about 3 minutes. Add remaining coconut milk. Stir to combine. Add blended ingredients. Stir well. Add to cooked rice.

Stir in bell pepper and soybeans. Salt & pepper to taste.

Garnish with the cilantro you set aside.

Baked Goods & Desserts

Island Naturals Granola	V	146
Scones	V	148
Jalapeño Cheddar Pull Aparts		150
Tapioca Pudding	V GF	152
Sweet Potato Tapioca Pudding	V GF	153
Vegan Banana Cake	V	154
Island Naturals Carrot Cake	V	155
Vegan Cream Cheese Frosting	V GF	157
Vegan Chocolate Frosting	V GF	158
Vegan Chocolate Cake	V	159
Raw Chocolate Truffles	V GF R	161
Vegan Date Squares	V GF	162
Raw Mint Marble Pie	V GF R	164
Summer Berry Purée	V GF R	167
Vegan Pumpkin Pie	V GF	168

ISLAND NATURALS GRANOLA

Store-bought granola does not compare to this personalized recipe. Once you go homemade, we bet that you will never go back. Place in quart jars to store or to give as gifts. Easily doubles.
Makes about 20 servings or 2 ½ lbs

    5 cups oats
    ½ cup wheat germ
    ½ cup sunflower seeds
    ½ cup almonds, whole or slivered
    ½ cup cashew pieces
    pinch of salt

    ¼ cup brown sugar
    ½ cup honey or agave nectar
    ½ cup safflower oil
    ½ tsp cinnamon
    ½ tsp vanilla

    ½ cup raisins
    ½ cup dried cranberries
    ½ cup date pieces

Combine the oats, wheat germ, sunflower seeds, almond, cashews and salt in large bowl. Set aside.

In a medium saucepan, add sugar, honey, oil, cinnamon and vanilla. Bring to a rolling boil over medium high heat. Stir constantly until thick, about 5 minutes.

Once thickened, mix into dry ingredients. Spread onto a rimmed baking sheet.

Bake at 325 degrees F for 10 minutes. Turn granola after 5 minutes. Remove from heat and let cool.

Add the raisins, cranberries, and dates to cooled granola. Store in an airtight container.

Tip: This recipe is highly adaptable to your personal tastes. Substitute anything you'd like. Try maple syrup for honey. Vary the spice. Put in your favorite nuts or fruits.

It's easy to make really big batches if your family eats lots of granola.

SCONES

Scones are a great treat for teatime, slow weekend mornings, or holidays. Of course, bake them the night before and you can make any morning a little more special with your favorite scone!
Yields 12 scones

- 4 cup unbleached organic flour
- 1 ½ cups raw sugar
- 1 ½ tbsp baking powder
- ½ tsp salt
- 1 cup natural butter substitute*, softened
- 1 cup total fruits or nuts or combination, chopped (optional)
- 1 cup soy milk

*We prefer Earth Balance brand Vegan Buttery Sticks

In a large mixing bowl, combine flour, sugar, baking powder and salt. Cut in natural butter substitute until a crumbly dough forms, resembling cornmeal.

Mix in your choice of fruits and nuts.

Slowly add soy milk, stirring until moist. Do not over mix. Consistency should be lumpy and thick like biscuit dough.

Scoop about a ¼ cup of dough onto a greased baking sheet, leaving about 3 inches between each.

Bake at 350 degrees F for 20 minutes or until golden brown. Do not over bake.

Tip: We recommend a little experimenting with add-ins. Try what you have on hand, what you know you like, or something off the cuff.

Any nut or seeds will do just fine in this recipe. Pick your favorite or try something new— macadamia nuts, pecans, walnuts, pistachios or almonds. Flax, sunflower and poppy seeds are delicious and nutritious additions too.

For the fullest flavor, dry roast the nuts or seeds for 10-15 minutes at 350 degrees F. Cool completely before chopping.

Fruits to consider include raisins, currants, dried apricots, dates, cranberries, blueberries, strawberries, or cherries…you get the idea. Fresh, frozen or dried is fine.

For a decadent treat, add chocolate chips or cacao nibs. Add ½ teaspoon fresh lemon or orange zest to compliment.

Some or our favorites add-ins are li'likoi, almonds and blueberries.

So, what's your favorite combination?

JALAPEÑO CHEDDAR PULL APARTS

These are notoriously addicting, so consider yourself warned! A delicious lunchbox treat or anytime snack.
Makes 12 pull aparts

3 cups lukewarm water
1 ½ tbsp yeast
¼ cup barley malt
7 – 8 cups flour
1 tbsp salt

½ lb cheddar cheese, cubed
¼ cup garlic, minced
½ red onion, chopped
1 bunch parsley, chopped
¼ cup + 1 tbsp olive oil
¼ cup jalapeño, diced (optional)

Add water to a large bowl, whisk in yeast and malt until dissolved.

Slowly add flour, ½ cup at a time. Stir in until dough starts to form. Add salt. Finish adding flour until the dough pulls away from the bowl and can be handled.

Place dough in an oiled bowl, cover and let rise for about 1 hour, until double in size.

Combine cheese, garlic, onion and parsley in a bowl and set aside.

When dough has doubled in size, punch down. On a floured surface, flatten dough into a rectangle about 1 inch thick. Cover with olive oil and cheese mixture. Fold the dough in half lengthwise to form a long skinny rectangle. Cut this into 6 strips lengthwise. Then cut the strips crosswise into cubes.

If using jalapeños, split dough cubes between two bowls. Add jalapeños to one bowl. Combine all cubes again.

Using your hands, form 12 equal sized portions. (These will not be uniform. Do not squish into a ball; simply get them to stick together.) Set on a baking sheet.

Let rise for 20 – 30 minutes.

Bake at 325 degrees F for 15 – 10 minutes or until golden brown and cheese is nicely melted.

Enjoy—and we know you will!

Tip: You can switch the savory for sweet. Try replacing the jalapeño and cheddar with apples and cinnamon and brie. Delicious!

TAPIOCA PUDDING

Tapioca pudding is a wonderfully satisfying treat without being too sweet. This may very well become a go-to recipe for you. Don't be shy about trying the sweet potato variety on the next page—it is scrumptious!
Serves 4

- 3 cups water
- ½ cup small pearl tapioca
- 2 ¼ cups (18 oz) unsweetened coconut milk
- ½ cup raw sugar
- ½ tsp vanilla (optional)

In a medium saucepan, bring water to a rolling boil. Add tapioca. Reduce heat to medium-high. Continue boiling for 7-10 minutes while stirring. Tapioca is done when pearls become translucent with no white coloring.

Turn off heat. Add coconut milk, sugar and vanilla. Stir well until sugar is dissolved. Pour into individual serving bowls and serve warm or refrigerate.

Tip: For an added treat, top with a sprinkle of nutmeg or cinnamon. For more flare, top with chopped peanuts or mango.

SWEET POTATO TAPIOCA PUDDING

Make this delicious tapioca pudding recipe using the directions on the previous page.
Serves 4

   1 hand size purple sweet potato, scrubbed clean

Prepare sweet potato. In a small saucepan, add enough water to cover sweet potato. Boil until tender, about 15 minutes.

Cool and peel.

In a small bowl, smash about a third of the cooked potato with a fork. Mix in a bit of the coconut milk until consistency of mashed potatoes.

Cut remaining 2/3 of potato into small cubes. Set aside.

Now begin recipe from previous page. Add both the smashed potato and cubes to tapioca when adding coconut milk, sugar and vanilla.

What a color and flavor!

VEGAN BANANA CAKE

You will be wishing for very ripe bananas to make this cake. It is moist and delicious. You'll go ape over it!
Yields 1 cake

   3 cups flour
   1 ½ cups raw sugar
   2 ½ tsp baking powder
   1 tsp baking soda
   ½ tsp salt
   1 cup natural butter substitute*
   3 cups very ripe banana, mashed (about 8 bananas)
   1 tsp vanilla
   ¾ - 1 cup soy milk

   *We use Earth Balance

Combine dry ingredients in a medium bowl (flour to salt). Set aside.

Beat together wet ingredients in a large bowl. It will be a bit lumpy due to the bananas.

Slowly add dry ingredients into wet mixing by hand or on low speed.

Pour batter into two greased 8 by 8 inch round pans.

Bake at 300 degrees F for about 30 minutes, or until golden brown and cake springs up to touch.

Let cool completely before frosting with Vegan Cream Cheese Frosting (pg 157).

Tip: This cake is very forgiving. If short on bananas compensate with a bit more milk.

ISLAND NATURALS CARROT CAKE

This is another Island Naturals classic. It's a crowd-pleaser for all ages. Makes great cupcakes or a layer cake, as well.
Yields 1 cake

- 4 cups flour
- 3 ½ cups sugar
- 2 tsp baking powder
- 2 tsp baking soda
- 2 tsp salt
- 1-2 tsp cinnamon
- 3 cups carrots, shredded
- 2 cups safflower oil
- ½ cup egg replacer + 2 ½ cups water, whisked together
- 1 cup walnuts, chopped

Combine dry ingredients (flour to cinnamon) in a large bowl.

Add carrot, oil, egg replacer mix and walnuts. Beat until just mixed. Do not over mix.

Pour into an oiled and floured (or lined) 10 x 14 inch baking dish, two 8 x 8 inch cake pans or a cupcake pan.

Bake at 350 degrees F for 50 – 60 minutes or until an inserted toothpick comes out clean.

Cool before frosting with Vegan Cream Cheese Frosting (pg 157).

VEGAN CREAM CHEESE FROSTING

Delicious and satisfying! Adjust the sweetness to your liking. This is ideal for our Island Naturals Carrot Cake and Banana Cake.
Frosts 1 layer cake or 24 cupcakes

- 8 oz non-dairy cream cheese*
- ½ cup natural butter substitute**
- 2 - 4 cups sifted powdered sugar, to taste
- 1 tsp vanilla

*We use 1 tub of Tofutti brand
**We use Earth Balance

Cream butter and cream cheese substitutes until fluffy.

Add sugar a bit at a time. Taste test for sweetness. Beat in vanilla until smooth and fluffy. Continue to beat until white in color (not yellow).

Tip: Try dusting frosted cake with cinnamon. For coconut lovers, toast 2 cups of shredded coconut and press into frosted cake. Imagine adding just a few drops of your favorite cooking essence to the frosting.

Try adding a splash of beet or carrot juice to finished frosting as a natural food coloring.

WHEAT-FREE CHOCOLATE CAKE

This fabulous cake will satisfy even the most profound cravings. It is light without giving up any of the satisfaction of chocolate indulgence.
Makes 1 cake or 24 cupcakes

3 ½ cups all purpose gluten free baking flour*
1 ½ cups raw sugar
¾ cup sucanat
½ cup cocoa powder
2 ½ tsp baking soda
½ tsp salt
1 cup safflower oil
3 tsp vanilla
3 ½ cups water
2 tbsp vinegar

*We use Bob's Red Mill

In a large mixing bowl, combine dry ingredients (from flour to salt) together.

Make a well in the center of the dry ingredients and slowly add the oil, vanilla and water. Mix well until smooth, removing any lumps. Add vinegar. Stir well and quickly.

Pour into a 9 x 13 inch oiled or lined pan. Bake at 325 degrees F for 40-45 minutes or until a toothpick comes out clean.

Cool before frosting.

VEGAN CHOCOLATE CAKE

Vegan-licious! Quick, easy and crowd-pleasing. This recipe is perfect as is and also welcoming to add-ins and frosting. Use our Cream Cheese Frosting to create the Island Naturals favorite Black and White Cupcakes.
Makes 1 cake or 24 cupcakes

- 3 cups flour
- 2 cups sugar
- ½ cup cocoa powder
- 2 tsp baking soda
- 1 tsp salt
- ¾ cup vegetable oil
- 1 tsp vanilla
- 2 cups water
- 2 tsp white vinegar

Combine dry ingredients (flour to salt) in large bowl.

Combine oil, vanilla and water in a medium bowl.

Mix wet ingredients into dry. Do not over mix. Add vinegar last, quickly stirring to distribute thoroughly. Pour into a greased or lined cake pan or cupcake pan.

Bake at 350 degrees F for 30 minutes or until a toothpick inserted comes out clean.

Serve warm or cool before frosting.

VEGAN CHOCOLATE FROSTING

A tried and true favorite for all—vegan or not. Amply frosts 1 cake or 24 cupcakes

   1 ½ cups natural butter substitute*
   1 ½ cups palm kernel oil (shortening)
   1 cup cocoa powder
   5 cup powdered sugar
   1 tbs. vanilla
   ½ tub (4 oz.) vegan cream cheese**

  *we us Earth Balance brand
  **we use Tofutti brand

In a mixing bowl or stand-up mixer, combine butter substitute and oil. Beat for 2 -3 minutes until combined.

Slowly add cocoa powder and powdered sugar with mixer on low. Continue to beat until light and fluffy.

When well combined, add vanilla and cream cheese, mix on medium low, scraping down bowl as needed.

Serve atop your favorite cake and cupcakes. Refrigerate to ensure the frosting holds its form.

Tip: Decorate your frosted dessert with fresh edible flowers or fresh berries.

RAW CHOCOLATE TRUFFLES

Oh, these are good! Very good! Make as special gifts for yourself or others.
Makes about 20 truffles

- 2 cups raw cashews
- ¾ cup raw cacao powder
- 1 cup raw cacao butter, grated and melted
- ½ cup agave nectar
- 1 cup water
- 1 tbsp lemon juice
- 3 tbsp coconut oil

- ¼ - ½ cup raw shredded coconut and/or raw cacao powder

Add ingredients from cashews to coconut oil to a blender and blend until smooth.

Spread onto a rimmed baking sheet or pan and place in freezer for 1 to 2 hours until firm.

Remove from freezer and roll into 1-inch balls using a melon baller or spoon. Roll in coconut and/or cacao powder and place on a serving plate.

Refrigerate until serving.

Tip: You may roll your truffles in any number of decadent topping. Try chopped goji berries, lavender flowers, finely chopped nuts, raw pumpkin seeds, cinnamon or cayenne. Anything goes.

VEGAN DATE SQUARES

These bars make a great dessert or snack. Very easy and hands-on!
Yields 24 2-inch bars

- ¼ cup egg replacer
- ½ cup soy milk
- 1 cup sucanat
- 1 tsp vanilla
- 1 tsp baking powder
- 1 tsp salt
- 1 cup flour
- 2 cups walnuts or other nuts, finely chopped
- 4 cups date pieces

In a large bowl, combine egg replacer, soy milk, sucanat, vanilla, baking powder and salt. Add flour, nuts and date pieces. Stir to combine.

This mixture will be gooey and hard to stir. Once combined, press evenly into a greased or lined 9 by 16 inch baking pan.

Rinse your hands with water to help keep the sticky off and to make pressing the dough easier.

Bake at 300 degrees F until golden brown and dry on top, about 25 to 30 minutes.

Cut into 2-inch squares right out of the oven. Keep in pan until cooled. Store in an airtight container.

RAW MINT MARBLE PIE

This is decadent! Certainly not for raw food enthusiasts only—everyone will enjoy this. Don't be scared off, it is quite easy and definitely worthwhile. Read through the whole recipe for all ingredients before you begin.
Makes one 9-inch pie, serves up to 12

For the crust
  1 ½ cup raw almonds
  ¼ cup cacao powder
  4 tbsp coconut oil
  ¼ cup grated + 3 tbsp melted cacao butter
  1 tsp fresh lemon juice
  1 ½ tbsp agave nectar

Grind almonds in a food processor until a flour like consistency. (Do not over process or you will make almond butter.) Add remaining ingredients and pulse until combined.

Press evenly into bottom of a 9-inch springform pan.

Set aside in refrigerator while you prepare the filling, as directed below.

Marble Pie Filling in 3 Parts

Bowl One
  2 cups raw cashews
  ½ cup cacao butter
  ½ cup coconut oil
  ¾ cup agave nectar
  1 ½ cups water
  1 tbsp fresh lemon juice
  _____

Blend all ingredients in a blender until smooth and transfer to bowl number one.

Bowl Two
  ¼ cup cacao powder
  3 tbsp water
  _____

Put cacao powder and water into the blender. Blend to combine. Add 1 cup of Bowl One puree. Blend again. Set aside in bowl two.

Bowl Three
  ½ cup firmly packed mint leaves
  1 tsp fresh lemon juice
  1 drop mint oil
  _____

As above, put mint, lemon juice and oil into blender. Blend briefly. Add 1 cup of Bowl One puree. Blend until smooth and put in bowl three.

To finish: You should have three bowls of different filling mixtures.

Pour Bowl One puree on top of the crust.

Now add Bowl Two puree. You want to create a marbling effect. To do this, pour the puree gently while moving your hand around so the mixture is distributed randomly within the Bowl One mixture.

Add Bowl Three in the same way that you did Bowl Two.

To ensure marbling, take a cocktail stick or a toothpick and lightly swirl puree around the top. Be careful not to overdo it—less is more in this case!

Freeze 1-2 hours, until solid. Defrost 15 minutes before serving. Dip knife in hot water to cut.

Tip: If the cacao butter begins to set in any of the three filling bowls, place that bowl in a glass bowl that has been filled with a bit of hot water.

This dessert is sure to delight!

SUMMER BERRY PURREE

This beautiful purée allows for a stellar presentation of the Marble Pie. It is equally amazing over chocolate cake, or anything chocolate...or most anything at all, for that matter!
Yields about 1 cup

    1 ½ c organic mixed berries, fresh or frozen
    1 tsp agave nectar
    ½ tsp vanilla extract

Blend all ingredients together until smooth. Strain through a sieve.

When serving on the Marble pie, drizzle the summer berry puree on the plate and decorate the cake with fresh, in season berries such as strawberries, raspberries and red currants.
Top the berries with a mint leave.

Wow!

VEGAN PUMPKIN PIE

Don't wait for Thanksgiving—enjoy this pumpkin pie tomorrow. This delicious pie sets up overnight in the refrigerator, so plan to make it the night before. A personal favorite!
Serves 6-8

1 9-inch piecrust

1 15-oz solid-packed canned pumpkin
1 cup soy milk
3/4 cup sugar
¼ cup cornstarch
½ tbsp molasses
1 tsp vanilla
1 tsp cinnamon
½ tsp salt
½ tsp ground ginger
½ tsp grated nutmeg
½ tsp ground allspice

Mix all ingredients together in a mixing bowl or blender, until smooth. Pour into unbaked piecrust set on a baking sheet.

Bake at 350 degrees F for 60 minutes or until center is set. Cover the edges with foil if they brown too quickly. Cool on a wire rack.

Refrigerate overnight before serving.

Add your favorite non-dairy whipped topping before serving.

Gluten-Free Option: Use a gluten-free cornstarch and piecrust.

Drinks & Smoothies

Ginger Juice	∨ GF	171
Lemon Grass Juice	∨ GF	172
Island Naturals Classic Smoothies:		173
Green Goo	∨ GF R	173
Berry Builder	∨ GF R	174
Immune Me	∨ GF R	174
Get Mental	∨ GF R	174
Energy Eruption	∨ GF R	175
Hot Cold Buster	∨ GF R	175
Chill Out	∨ GF R	175
Jungle Jive	∨ GF R	176
Create Your Own	∨ GF R	176

GINGER JUICE

This juice is a refreshing alternative to soda with the added benefits of a healthy dose of ginger. Adjust quantity as needed.
Yields about 1 gallon

- ¾ cup ginger, peeled and chopped
- 1 gallon drinking water
- ½ - 1 cup raw sugar, more or less, to taste

Place ginger in a blender and blend until smooth. Add a little water for easier blending.

In a large saucepan, add the gallon of water and blended ginger. Bring to a boil, then turn down to simmer for 15 minutes. Remove from heat and cool until warm to touch.

Using cheesecloth or a fine mesh strainer, strain. Discard ginger. Add sugar and stir until dissolved.

Refrigerate overnight. The next day, adjust sweetness to taste. To add more sugar, first dissolve sugar in warm water then add a tablespoon at a time to desired sweetness.

Serve cold.

Tip: For Ginger Lime Juice, add ¼ cup fresh lime juice before refrigerating.

LEMONGRASS JUICE

A satisfying thirst quencher. This flies off our shelves!
Yields about 1 ½ gallons

- 10 pieces of lemongrass
- 2 oz kaffir lime leaves, washed
- 1 gallon drinking water
- 1 cup raw sugar, more or less, to taste
- ½ cup fresh lime juice

Cut the lemongrass stems about halfway up. Cut off bottom end and remove the tough outer leaves. Pound the stem lightly. (This "bruising" will allow the release of its flavors.)

In a large pot, add the lemongrass, kefir lime leaves and water. Bring to a boil, then turn down to simmer for 15 minutes. Remove from heat. Let stand until warm to touch.

Using cheesecloth or a fine mesh strainer, strain. Discard the lemongrass and lime leaves. Add sugar and stir until dissolved.

Refrigerate overnight. The next day, add the lime juice. Stir well.

Serve cold.

ISLAND NATURALS CLASSIC SMOOTHIES

The Island Naturals Classic Smoothies are blends that you can count on to please your palate and satisfy your hunger. Use all organic ingredients for your smoothies, just like we do.
Yields a 16 oz smoothie

To prepare smoothies, simply add liquid ingredients to a blender followed by remaining ingredients. Give it a good whirl to ensure a refreshing and smooth texture.

GREEN GOO

Spinach is for Popeye what the Green Goo Smoothie is for you. And it tastes great!

   8-10 oz apple juice
   3 ½ oz frozen bananas
   3 ½ oz frozen mango
   1 tsp spirulina
   ½ tsp bee pollen

BERRY BUILDER

Protein-rich and berry delicious, the Berry Builder is great any time of day.

   8-10 oz apple juice
   1 tbsp soy protein powder
   4 oz frozen bananas
   3 ½ oz mixed berries

IMMUNE ME

When everyone at work or school is coughing, sniffling and sneezing, try this immune boosting smoothie to keep yourself well.

   8-10 oz orange juice
   3 ½ oz frozen mango
   3 ½ oz frozen strawberry
   1 dropper echinacea tincture

GET MENTAL

Need to be extra sharp today? Try a Get Mental smoothie to kick that brain into high function.

   8-10 oz apple juice
   3 ½ oz frozen bananas
   3 ½ oz frozen strawberries
   1 dropper ginkgo tincture

ENERGY ERUPTION

Need a lift today? Try an Energy Eruption smoothie and you'll be rearing to go.

- 8-10 oz apple juice
- 3 ½ oz frozen bananas
- 3 ½ oz frozen strawberries
- 1 dropper ginseng tincture

HOT COLD BUSTER

When that head or sinus cold has you in its grips, stay in the fight with this smoothie. I have made special trips to Island Naturals for this smoothie. It helps!

- 8-10 oz lemon- ginger juice
- 3 ½ oz frozen pineapple
- 3 ½ oz frozen mango
- 1 dropper echinacea tincture
- Dash or pinch of cayenne pepper

CHILL OUT

Take the edge off your day with this smoothie.

- 8-10 oz coconut-pineapple juice
- 3 ½ oz frozen mango
- 3 ½ oz frozen strawberries
- 1 dropper kava tincture

JUNGLE JIVE

Refresh yourself with the Jungle Jive, with its healthful Hawaiian tonic, noni juice.

   8-10 oz apple juice
   3 ½ oz frozen mango
   3 ½ oz frozen pineapple
   1 oz noni juice

CREATE YOUR OWN

Feeling creative in the kitchen? Of course you are! Try combining your choice of the following ingredients to create your ultimate smoothie.

   3 ½ oz each of two fruits, fresh or frozen:
      banana, acai, strawberry, mango, papaya, pineapple, mixed berries

   8-10 oz of a liquid base:
      apple juice, coconut-pineapple juice, lemon ginger juice, soy milk, rice milk

   Additional add-ins, choice one or more:
      1 dropper of echinacea, ginseng, gingko or kava
      1 oz noni juice, spirulina, bee pollen or chia seeds
      2 tbsp cacao, yogurt, peanut butter, protein powder or goji berries

INDEX

A

Appetizers
- Artichoke Spinach Dip · 30
- Bruschetta · 32
- Chimichurri · 33
- Hummus · 24
- Mushroom pate · 25
- Olive Tapenade · 31
- Roasted Bell Pepper Tapenade · 26
- Roasted Red Pepper Tofu Dip · 29
- Salsa · 27
- Vegan Guacamole · 28

B

Baked Goods
- Island Naturals Carrot Cake · 155
- Island Naturals Granola · 146
- Jalapeno Cheddar Pull Aparts · 150
- Scones · 1–176
- Vegan Banana Cake · 154
- Vegan Chocolate Cake · 159
- Vegan Date Squares · 162
- Vegan Pumpkin Pie · 168

C

Chicken Dishes
- Chicken Enchiladas · 95
- Chicken Katsu · 102
- Chicken Mole · 109
- Coconut Chicken · 98
- Indian Chicken Curry · 103
- Island Naturals Lau Lau · 119
- Sherry Chicken · 107
- Tandoori Chicken · 100
- Thai Chicken Satay · 105

D

Desserts
- Island Naturals Carrot Cake · 155
- Raw Chocolate Truffles · 161
- Raw Mint Marble Pie · 164
- Summer Berry Puree · 167
- Sweet Potato Tapioca Pudding ·153
- Tapioca Pudding · 152
- Vegan Banana Cake · 154
- Vegan Chocolate Cake · 159
- Vegan Chocolate Frosting · 158
- Vegan Cream Cheese Frosting · 157
- Vegan Date Squares · 162
- Vegan Pumpkin Pie · 168

Dips
- Artichoke Spinach Dip · 30
- Bruschetta · 32
- Chimichurri · 33
- Hummus · 24
- Mushroom pate · 25
- Olive Tapenade · 31
- Roasted Bell Pepper Tapenade · 26
- Roasted Red Pepper Tofu Dip · 29
- Salsa · 27
- Vegan Guacamole · 28

Dressings

Flax Seed Oil Dressing · 3
Ginger Mint Dressing · 4
Oil-Less Dressing · 5

Drinks
Ginger Juice · 171
Lemongrass Juice · 172
Smoothies · *See* Smoothies

E

Entrees
Calzones · 130
Chicken Enchiladas · 95
Chicken Katsu · 102
Chicken Mole · 109
Coconut Chicken · 98
Fish Stew · 113
Goma-Dare Tofu · 132
Indian Chicken Curry · 103
Eggplant Parmesan · 122
Island Naturals Alaskan Salmon · 112
Island Naturals Lau Lau · 119
Lasagna · 124
Moroccan Stew · 128
Pad Thai · 133
Salmon Croquettes · 117
Savory Tofu · 126
Sherry Chicken · 107
Stuffed Bell Peppers · 115
Tandoori Chicken · 100
Thai Chicken Satay · 105
Turkey Meat Loaf · 110

F

Fish Dishes
Fish Stew · 113
Island Naturals Alaskan Salmon · 112
Island Naturals Lau Lau · 119
Salmon Croquettes · 117
Stuffed Bell Peppers · 115

G

Gluten Free
Ancho Chili Sauce · 12
Artichoke Spinach Dip · 30
Asian Rice Pilaf · 137
Beets Salad · 35
Berry Builder · 174
Cashew Gravy · 22
Chicken Enchiladas · 95
Chicken Mole · 109
Chill Out · 1175
Chimichurri · 33
Coconut Chicken · 98
Creamy Leek Soup · 63
Create Your Own Smoothie · 176
Delightful Lima Bean Soup · 67
Dill Marinade · 8
Dill Potato Salad · 38
Eggplant Parmesan · 122
Eggplant Pockets · 81
Energy Eruption · 175
Fiesta Bean Salad · 48
Flax Seed Oil Dressing · 3
Garlic Chili Marinade · 8
Garlic Rosemary Roasted Potatoes · 136
Get Mental · 174
Ginger Juice · 171
Ginger Mint Dressing · 4
Goma-Dare Tofu · 132
Greek Pasta Salad · 41
Green Goo · 173
Green Papaya Salad · 44
Heart of Palm Salad · 52
Hijiki Seaweed Salad · 47
Hot Cold Buster · 175
Hummus · 24
Immune Me · 174
Indian Chicken Curry · 103
Indian Potato Soup · 55

Island Naturals Alaskan Salmon · 112
Island Naturals Fry Rice · 140
Island Naturals Lau Lau · 119
Island Sweet Potato Salad · 40
Jungle Jive · 176
Lasagna · 124
Lemongrass Juice · 172
Mac Nut Ahi Poke · 82
Marinara Sauce · 14
Mexican Rice · 142
Miso Soup · 66
Mix Bean Salad · 49
Moroccan Stew · 128
Mushroom Pate · 25
Nori Shoyu Marinade · 10
Oil-Less Dressing · 5
Olive Tapenade · 31
Pad Thai · 133
Pasta Salad · 42
Peanut Sauce · 17
Pesto · 16
Pickled Papaya Salad · 45
Polenta Pizza · 79
Quinoa Salad · 50
Quinoa Soup · 57
Raw Chocolate Truffles · 161
Raw Mint Marble Pie · 164
Roasted Bell Pepper Tapenade · 26
Roasted Red Pepper Tofu Dip · 29
Salsa · 27
Savory Tofu · 126
Seaweed Ahi Poke · 82
Seaweed Salad · 46
Shiitake Mushroom Marinade · 7
Spring Rolls · 72
Summer Berry Puree · 167
Summer Rolls · 77
Sweet & Sour Sauce · 20
Sweet Chili Sauce · 18
Sweet Potato Tapioca Pudding · 153
Tabouli · 53
Tandoori Chicken · 100
Tapioca Pudding · 152
Teriyaki Sauce · 19
Thai Chicken Satay · 105
Thai Curry Rice · 143
Thai Peanut Marinade · 9
Thai Tofu Salad · 84
Tofu Poke · 83
Turkey Meat Loaf · 110
Vegan Chocolate Frosting · 158
Vegan Cream Cheese Frosting · 157
Vegan Guacamole · 28
Vegan Potato Salad · 39
Vegan Pumpkin Pie · 168
Vegan Southern-Style Gravy · 21
Warabi Salad · 51
Gravies
Cashew Gravy · 22
Vegan Southern-Style Gravy · 21

L

Light Fare
Eggplant Pockets · 81
Mac Nut Ahi Poke · 82
Polenta Pizza · 79
Seaweed Ahi Poke · 82
Spring Rolls · 72
Summer Rolls · 77
Thai Tofu Salad · 84
Tofu Meatless Balls · 73
Tofu Nuggets · 75
Tofu Poke · 83
Walnut Tofu Balls · 74

M

Marinades
Dill Marinade · 8
Garlic Chili Marinade · 8

Honey Dijon Marinade · 9
Nori Shoyu Marinade · 10
Shiitake Mushroom Marinade · 7
Thai Peanut Marinade · 9

R

Raw Foods
    Berry Builder · 174
    Chill Out · 175
    Create Your Own Smoothie · 176
    Energy Eruption · 174
    Get Mental · 174
    Ginger Juice · 171
    Green Goo · 173
    Green Papaya Salad · 44
    Heart of Palm Salad · 52
    Hijiki Seaweed Salad · 47
    Hot Cold Buster · 175
    Immune Me · 174
    Jungle Jive · 176
    Mac Nut Ahi Poke · 82
    Pickled Papaya Salad · 45
    Raw Chocolate Truffles · 161
    Raw Mint Marble Pie · 164
    Seaweed Ahi Poke · 82
    Summer Berry Puree · 167

S

Salads
    Beets Salad ·35
    Cold Noodle Salad · 36
    Couscous Salad · 37
    Dill Potato Salad · 38
    Fiesta Bean Salad · 48
    Greek Pasta Salad · 41
    Green Papaya Salad · 44
    Heart of Palm Salad · 52
    Hijiki Seaweed Salad · 47
    Island Sweet Potato Salad · 40
    Mix Bean Salad · 49
    Pasta Salad · 42
    Pickled Papaya Salad · 45
    Quinoa Salad · 50
    Seaweed Salad · 46
    Tabouli Salad · 53
    Vegan Potato Salad · 39
    Warabi Salad · 51
Sauces
    Ancho Chili Sauce · 12
    Marinara Sauce · 14
    Peanut Sauce · 17
    Pesto · 16
    Sweet & Sour Sauce · 20
    Sweet Chili Sauce · 18
    Teriyaki Sauce · 19
Side Dishes
    Asian Rice Pilaf · 137
    Garlic Rosemary Roasted Potatoes · 136
    Island Naturals Fry Rice · 140
    Mexican Rice · 142
    Thai Curry Rice · 143
Smoothies
    Berry Builder · 174
    Chill Out · 175
    Create Your Own · 176
    Energy Eruption · 175
    Get Mental · 174
    Green Goo · 173
    Hot Cold Buster · 175
    Immune Me · 174
    Island Naturals Classic Smoothies · 173
    Jungle Jive · 176
Soups
    Creamy Leek Soup · 63
    Delightful Lima Bean Soup · 67
    Indian Potato Soup · 55
    Miso Soup · 66
    Mushroom Barley Soup · 69
    Quinoa Soup · 57
    Vegan Corn Chowder · 59

Vegan Ham & Bean Soup · 62
Vegan Potato Leek Soup · 65

T

Tofu
    Goma-Dare Tofu · 132
    Pad Thai · 133
    Roasted Red Pepper Tofu Dip · 29
    Savory Tofu · 126
    Summer Rolls · 77
    Thai Tofu Salad · 84
    Tofu Meatless Balls · 73
    Tofu Nuggets · 75
    Tofu Poke · 83
    Vegan Corn Chowder · 59
    Vegan Potato Leek Soup · 65
    Walnut Tofu Balls · 74

V

Vegan
    Ancho Chili Sauce · 12
    Asian Rice Pilaf · 137
    Beets Salad · 35
    Berry Builder · 174
    Bruschetta · 32
    Cashew Gravy · 22
    Chill Out · 175
    Chimichurri · 33
    Cold Noodle Salad · 36
    Couscous Salad · 37
    Creamy Leek Soup · 63
    Create Your Own Smoothie · 176
    Delightful Lima Bean Soup · 67
    Dill Potato Salad · 38
    Eggplant Pockets · 81
    Energy Eruption · 175
    Fiesta Bean Salad · 48
    Flax Seed Oil Dressing · 3
    Garlic Chili Marinade · 8
    Garlic Rosemary Roasted Potatoes · 136
    Get Mental · 174
    Ginger Juice · 171
    Ginger Mint Dressing · 14
    Goma-Dare Tofu · 132
    Greek Pasta Salad · 41
    Green Goo · 173
    Green Papaya Salad · 44
    Heart of Palm Salad · 52
    Hijiki Seaweed Salad · 47
    Honey Dijon Marinade · 9
    Hot Cold Buster · 175
    Hummus · 24
    Immune Me · 174
    Indian Potato Soup · 55
    Island Naturals Carrot Cake · 155
    Island Naturals Fry Rice ·140
    Island Naturals Granola · 146
    Island Sweet Potato Salad · 40
    Jungle Jive · 176
    Lemongrass Juice · 172
    Marinara Sauce · 14
    Mexican Rice · 142
    Miso Soup · 66
    Mix Bean Salad · 49
    Moroccan Stew · 128
    Mushroom Barley Soup · 69
    Mushroom Pate · 25
    Nori Shoyu Marinade · 10
    Oil-Less Dressing · 5
    Olive Tapenade · 31
    Pad Thai · 133
    Pasta Salad · 42
    Peanut Sauce · 17
    Pickled Papaya Salad · 45
    Quinoa Salad · 50
    Quinoa Soup · 57
    Raw Chocolate Truffles · 161

Raw Mint Marble Pie · 164
Roasted Red Pepper Tofu Dip · 29
Salsa · 27
Savory Tofu · 126
Scones · 148
Seaweed Salad · 46
Shiitake Mushroom Marinade · 7
Spring Rolls · 72
Summer Berry Puree · 167
Summer Rolls · 77
Sweet & Sour Sauce · 20
Sweet Chili Sauce · 18
Sweet Potato Tapioca Pudding · 153
Tabouli · 53
Tapioca Pudding · 152
Teriyaki Sauce · 19
Thai Curry Rice · 143
Thai Peanut Marinade · 9
Thai Tofu Salad · 84
Tofu Meatless Balls · 73
Tofu Nuggets · 75
Tofu Poke · 83
Vegan Banana Cake · 154
Vegan Chocolate Cake · 159
Vegan Chocolate Frosting · 158
Vegan Corn Chowder · 59
Vegan Cream Cheese Frosting · 157
Vegan Date Squares · 162
Vegan Guacamole · 28
Vegan Ham & Bean Soup · 62
Vegan Potato Leek Soup · 65
Vegan Potato Salad · 39
Vegan Pumpkin Pie · 168
Vegan Southern-Style Gravy · 21
Walnut Tofu Balls · 74
Warabi Salad · 51

ACKNOWLEDGMENTS

Special thanks to Ritsuko Tokura-Ellsworth, Rose Bryenton and Wannapha "Oy" Lionheart for developing the recipes in this book. Thanks to past chefs, Joshua Ketner and Marshall Freitas.

The following brave home chefs were infinitely helpful in downsizing recipes from quantities to feed a hungry Hawaiian town to feeding your family. Many thanks to Amy, Eli, Dropati, Chris, Cindy, Colin, Dayne, Kelsey and Ryan.

A warm thank you to Russell for, well, Island Naturals and his loving support during the making of this book.

My admiration and thanks to Patricia Leo for her beautiful artwork. The mural at Island Naturals Kona is a must-see, one of the nicest works of art on this Island!

Love and thanks to Zoe for her wonderful drawings throughout these pages. She is also one of the two best daughters ever!

Love and thanks to Grace, the other best daughter—I will send you a copy!

Thank *you* for purchasing this book and creating wholesome, delicious meals at home for your family and friends.

Here's to good food and good health!
—Gina

This book is printed on recycled paper.